Trends and Drivers of Agri-environmental Performance in OECD Countries

This document, as well as any data and map included herein, are without prejudice to the status of or sovereignty over any territory, to the delimitation of international frontiers and boundaries and to the name of any territory, city or area.

The statistical data for Israel are supplied by and under the responsibility of the relevant Israeli authorities. The use of such data by the OECD is without prejudice to the status of the Golan Heights, East Jerusalem and Israeli settlements in the West Bank under the terms of international law.

Please cite this publication as:
OECD (2019), *Trends and Drivers of Agri-environmental Performance in OECD Countries*, OECD Publishing, Paris, *https://doi.org/10.1787/b59b1142-en*.

ISBN 978-92-64-38291-6 (print)
ISBN 978-92-64-31983-7 (pdf)

Foreword

Agriculture is facing a key challenge in reducing its impact on the environment, including preserving vital natural resources such as soil and water. For more than 20 years, the OECD has been tracking the agriculture sector's environmental impact, collecting information against more than 60 agri-environmental indicators (AEIs) in its member countries. Over time, this geographical coverage has expanded to include Argentina, Brazil, Bulgaria, the People's Republic of China, Colombia, Costa Rica, Croatia, Cyprus, Indonesia, India, Kazakhstan, Malta, the Philippines, Romania, Russian Federation, South Africa, Ukraine, and Viet Nam.

This report updates the data published in the 2015 OECD Compendium of Agri-environmental Indicators to present a summary of the environmental performance of agriculture in OECD countries as of end-2015. The report also includes new and innovative material to further strengthen its relevance as a reference document. In particular, the four thematic chapters each cover a targeted set of indicators for which data coverage is generally more consistent across time in OECD countries and that capture the main pressures agriculture exerts on the environment. Chapter 1 focuses on the interlinked issues of land use, pesticides and farmland birds; Chapter 2 covers ammonia and greenhouse gas emissions, the main air pollutants from agricultural activities; Chapter 3 is dedicated to nitrogen and phosphorus balances, two indicators that signal air and water pollution; and Chapter 4 focuses on water use and irrigation.

In addition to summarising the main trends in these selected AEIs, each chapter also identifies the main drivers of the observed trends based, for Chapters 1 to 3, on econometric analyses using the OECD AEIs.

The report recognises the difficulties in developing a comparative set of agri-environmental indicators given that methodologies to measure indicators are not well established in all cases and may differ across countries. National-level data can conceal significant ranges, reflecting local site-specific values, and year-to-year variations in the value of indicators may reflect weather variability. To minimise these problems, the report focuses on long-term trends and supports the findings with empirical evidence from the literature.

Finally, all chapters discuss country cases and distil policy lessons on how to improve the environmental performance of the agriculture sector.

This report was declassified by the OECD Joint Working Party on Agriculture and the Environment (JWPAE), of the OECD Committee for Agriculture and the OECD Environment Policy Committee.

Acknowledgements

The OECD wishes to thanks its member countries for their collaboration and contributions in the preparation of this report, in particular through the provision of data and expert comments on the text. The very useful information provided by Ebba Barany from Eurostat and Panos Panagos from the Joint Research Centre; the European Bird Census Council; the Food and Agriculture Organization of the United Nations (FAO); the UN Environment Programme; and the UN Framework Convention on Climate Change are also appreciated.

The principal author of this report is Santiago Guerrero, Policy Analyst in the Agriculture and Resources Policies Division of the OECD Trade and Agriculture Directorate. The following analysts co-authored Chapters 1, 2, 3 and 4 respectively: Alea Muñoz, Maho Nakagawa, Iván Tzuntzín, and Julien Hardelin. Many colleagues from the Trade and Agriculture Directorate and the Environment Directorate also contributed to this report, in particular Franck Jesus, Guillaume Gruère, Dimitris Diakosavvas, Katia Karousakis, and Will Symes. This report also benefitted from the statistical assistance of Noura Takrouri-Jolly, Karine Souvanheuane, and Véronique de Saint-Martin. Michèle Patterson prepared this report for publication and Theresa Poincet provided administrative support.

Table of contents

Tables

Figures

Boxes

Acronyms

BMPs	Best Management Practices
BPA	Biodiversity Promotion Areas (Switzerland)
CAP	Common Agricultural Policy (European Union)
CH_4	Methane
CO_2	Carbon Dioxide
CLRTAP	Convention on Long-Range Transboundary Air Pollution
EEF	Enhanced Efficiency Fertiliser
EOA	Environmental Objectives of Agriculture (Switzerland)
EQIP	Environmental Quality Incentives Program (United States)
ETS	Emissions Trading Scheme (New Zealand)
ESAs	Environmentally Sensitive Areas (Denmark)
EU	European Union
GDP	Gross Domestic Product
GHG	Greenhouse Gas Emissions
GIS	Geographic Information Systems
GPS	Global Positioning Systems
N	Nitrogen
N_2O	Nitrous Oxide
NH_3	Ammonia
NO_3	Nitrate
NO	Nitric Oxide
NO_x	Nitrogen Oxides
NTIC	New Technologies of Information and Communication
NVZ	Nitrate Vulnerable Zones
P	Phosphorus
PM	Particulate Matter
PSE	Producer Support Estimate
SO_2	Sulphur Dioxide
TFP	Total Factor Productivity
UNECE	United Nations Economic Commission for Europe
VOCs	Volatile Organic Compounds

Executive Summary

The environmental performance of the agriculture sector registered some improvement in OECD countries during the period 2003-15, notwithstanding some signs of stagnation in particular areas. The majority of OECD countries saw decreasing trends in ammonia emissions, phosphorus surplus and water abstraction rates. Results were more mixed for nitrogen balances, which, while declining on average, nevertheless, increased in several countries, including in some with already high nitrogen surplus levels. A lack of progress was also observed in reducing greenhouse gas emissions and on improving biodiversity on farmland. Greenhouse gas emissions increased slightly in the OECD region, while the farmland birds' indicator, the main OECD indicator used to track biodiversity on farmland, continued to decline in the majority of countries for which monitoring was undertaken. Overall, improvements in the environmental performance of the agricultural sector slowed down during the period 2003-15, relative to the pace observed over the period 1993-2005.

These developments occurred in a context where agricultural land area and support to farmers declined and agricultural production increased in OECD countries. In the period 2002-15, both croplands and grasslands were converted to other uses; the area of cropland was transformed into tree-covered areas or artificial surfaces, such as buildings and roads, while the area of grasslands was transformed to sparse vegetation and tree-covered areas. There were also regional variations in land conversion: in European OECD countries, croplands and grasslands were mainly converted to tree-covered areas, while in the Asian and Oceanian OECD countries, cropland conversion was dominated by artificial surfaces and grassland conversion by sparse vegetation. In most OECD countries, the decline in agricultural land was accompanied by an expansion of agriculture production.

Over the 2003-15 period, agricultural policies in OECD countries changed substantially: support to farmers relative to gross farm receipts declined from nearly 30% in 2003 to 17% in 2015, and the majority of OECD countries reformed their support policies to increase the share of payments decoupled from production or input use. In addition, most OECD countries made direct payments conditional on compliance with environmental regulations and established agri-environmental payments schemes that paid farmers to improve the environmental performance of their farms.

These policy reforms improved the environmental performance of agriculture. The empirical analysis conducted for this report finds that replacing distortionary forms of support – such as market price support and subsidies linked to input or production – with support which is not linked to current production, inputs or area of production tends to decrease nitrogen and phosphorus surpluses. Likewise, designing policies and regulations to target specific forms of pollution, such as the Nitrates Directive in the European Union, decreased both nitrogen and phosphorous surpluses. Implementing agri-environmental schemes that provide payments for areas set aside or that specifically target the conservation of high ecological value areas was also shown to effectively improve the biodiversity on farmland.

Contextual and external factors are important drivers of the environmental performance of agriculture. In particular, the crop mix and livestock population and herd composition play a strong role. In countries where the cultivated area with oil crops increased or where cattle stocks declined, both nitrogen and phosphorus surpluses decreased. In countries where irrigated corn area was replaced with other crops, water abstraction rates declined. Oil crops are positively associated with the prevalence of farmland birds; in contrast, hotter temperatures and higher insecticide use per hectare are negatively associated with farmland birds.

The report also explores the relationship between labour productivity and greenhouse gas emission intensities (kg CO_2/USD), as well as the potential of emerging technologies to improve the environmental performance of agriculture. In OECD countries, growth in agricultural labour productivity is concomitant with GHG emission intensity reductions only up to a certain point, after which emission intensities no longer decrease and may even increase. Indeed, OECD countries may be reaching a point at which further productivity improvements may not be enough to reduce GHG emissions per unit of output.

Technological innovations, such as geographic information systems, global positioning systems, remote sensors, in situ sensors, yield monitoring, and variable rate technologies used in precision agriculture have the potential to improve the environmental performance of agriculture by targeting chemical input applications and saving energy. Enhanced efficiency nitrogen fertilisers can improve crop uptake of nitrogen and reduce the risk of nitrogen leaching. The ultimate environmental impact of these technologies is, however, highly dependent upon the type of crop and the biophysical conditions of the farm, as well as on other management practices. Adoption of efficient irrigation techniques has the potential to reduce water abstraction rates, but increased efficiency may also have negative environmental consequences such as lower groundwater recharging rates.

Monitoring agricultural indicators – and in particular measuring the environmental impact of agriculture – across OECD countries continues to be challenging, given the difficulties in developing a set of agri-environmental indicators that are comparable across countries and consistent through time. The integration of digital technologies into monitoring programmes, in particular, could improve the accuracy of agri-environmental indicators and the geographical scale at which they are measured.

1. Land use, pesticides and biodiversity in farmland

This chapter analyses recent trends in agricultural land use, farmland bird biodiversity and pesticide sales indicators in OECD countries, considering their linkages and the role of specific agri-environmental policies. It also discusses how Switzerland is addressing biodiversity loss on farmland.

The statistical data for Israel are supplied by and under the responsibility of the relevant Israeli authorities. The use of such data by the OECD is without prejudice to the status of the Golan Heights, East Jerusalem and Israeli settlements in the West Bank under the terms of international law.

Key messages

- Agricultural land area continued to decline in the majority of OECD countries, particularly those in Western Europe, over the period 2002-14. The rate of decline accelerated when compared to the previous decade. Nevertheless, agricultural production increased in the OECD area, signalling an increase in land productivity.

- In countries where permanent cropland is a significant share of total agricultural land, pesticide sales per hectare were significantly higher than the OECD average. Fungicides are the most common pesticides sold in OECD countries (37% of all pesticides), followed by herbicides (32%).

- The farmland bird index, an indicator of the biodiversity of farmland birds, continued to decline over the period 2002-14 in almost all OECD countries monitoring this indicator, and at an accelerated rate.

- The key factors for this trend are: increased use of insecticides per hectare; loss of landscape heterogeneity, particularly the extent of crop fields without trees, bushes and other woody elements; and hotter temperatures.

- At the country level, agri-environmental support policies that tend to improve farmland bird populations are those that decouple support from production, e.g. provide payments for areas set aside or specifically target the conservation of high ecological value areas, wildlife or biodiversity. An econometric analysis of 22 countries suggests that agri-environmental support policies are less effective at improving biodiversity when coupled with input use or production, such as those that impose environmental constraints or environmentally friendly practices on the production of a specific commodity or the use of specific inputs.

- The net positive impact on biodiversity of agri-environmental policies is not clear. The reason is that such policies can decrease yields and production in the country where they are adopted, which in turn can stimulate land conversion to agricultural uses and higher production in other countries, potentially affecting areas with high biodiversity.

- The example of Switzerland illustrates that both the quantity of set-aside areas and ecological quality are important to improving biodiversity. In particular, improving the quality of set-aside areas can have large benefits for biodiversity, especially for farmland birds. The amount of high-quality set-aside areas on farms (6.3% of agricultural land) in Switzerland needs to be increased, however, in order to maximise the effect of set-aside areas on the farmland bird population, particularly for those species at risk and which have specific needs in terms of habitat.

1.1. Interactions between land use, pesticide use and biodiversity

There is widespread evidence that biodiversity on farmland is declining globally (Landis, 2017[1]). Declines in the diversity of plants (Kleijn et al., 2012[2]; José-María et al., 2011[3]), birds (Landis, 2017[1]; Donald, Green and Heath, 2001[4]; Donald et al., 2006[5]; Stanton, Morrissey and Clark, 2018[6]; Chamberlain et al., 2000[7]) pollinators (Potts et al., 2010[8]; Bartomeus et al., 2013[9]), and insects in general (Sánchez-Bayo and Wyckhuys, 2019[10]) have been documented, mainly in North America and Europe.

Multiple ecosystem services are potentially affected are potentially affected by biodiversity loss, many of them relevant to agriculture (Díaz et al., 2006[11]; Mace, Norris and Fitter, 2012[12]). These include regulating services such as nutrient cycle regulation, pollination, pest control, climate regulation and seed dispersal; provisioning services such as crop, livestock and medicine production; and cultural services such as landscape amenities for recreation or contemplation (Mace, Norris and Fitter, 2012[12]; Hardelin and Lankoski, 2018[13]). For example, notwithstanding the different approaches to measuring pollinator dependency of crops, pollinators are estimated to contribute to the pollination of three-quarters of the main cultivated crops worldwide (Hardelin and Lankoski, 2018[13]), sustaining the production of many fruits, vegetables and seeds. Soil biodiversity – bacteria, fungi and earthworms – can improve the efficiency of water and nitrogen use (de Ruiter and Brown, 2007[14]), and insects can provide biological pest control (Hardelin and Lankoski, 2018[13]). These ecosystem services are relevant at different scales: field, farm, landscape, regional and global (Hardelin and Lankoski, 2018[13]).

Changes in land and pesticide use are key drivers of change in farmland biodiversity, particularly farmland birds (Stanton, Morrissey and Clark, 2018[6]; OECD, 2018[15]). Excess nutrient applications can negatively impact biodiversity due to increased toxicity in the environment and nutrient enrichment, oxygen depletion in aquatic ecosystems, soil or water acidification, or by multiplying the impact of other stressors such as pathogens, invasive species, and climate change (OECD, 2018[15]). Declines in agricultural land area, loss of crop diversity, landscape heterogeneity (the combination of different land uses in a given space), and greater use of chemical inputs – all symptoms of the intensification of agriculture – are some of the main pressures faced by farmland birds in most OECD countries (Firbank et al., 2008[16]; Tilman et al., 2001[17]). It should be noted that the habitat quality for promoting farmland biodiversity also depends on the type of crops grown (Jerrentrup et al., 2017[18]; Turley, 2006[19]).

The intensification of agricultural activities can reduce biodiversity but so does the expansion of the agricultural frontier. The latter has occurred mainly in tropical countries, where more than 80% of forest clearings over the last 30 years have been attributed to agriculture, for both subsistence and commercial purposes (Hosonuma et al., 2012[20]). While this expansion has contributed little to global production due to low yields, its environmental impact on biodiversity loss, greenhouse gas emissions, and soil degradation has been significant (Foley et al., 2011[21]).

Biodiversity both within farmland and in natural areas will continue to be at risk due to increased food production to satisfy rising global demand for crops and food, which is expected to grow at 1% per year over the coming decade (OECD/FAO, 2018[22]). To satisfy global food demand, arable lands are likely to expand in South America, Sub-Saharan Africa, and South East Asia, increasing pressure on natural habitats and ecosystems in those regions, while the intensification process of agriculture is expected to continue to increase mainly in Europe (OECD/FAO, 2018[22]), exacerbating environmental challenges associated with agricultural activities in Europe.

1.2. Trends in land use, pesticides and biodiversity indicators

In view of the connection between the biodiversity on farmland, land use and pesticides, this chapter focuses on three agri-environmental indicators: land area, pesticide use and biodiversity (Annex 1.B).[1]

Agricultural land area continues to shrink in OECD countries, while agricultural production increases

Agricultural land is declining in most OECD countries, with the rate of decline accelerating over the 2002-14 period. The exceptions were Chile, Estonia, Finland, Greece, Ireland, Latvia, Luxembourg, Mexico, and the United States. In most countries where agricultural land has been shrinking, the rate of decline was faster during 2002-14 than during 1992-2004 Figure 1.1). From 2004 to 2015, lost cropland in OECD countries was mainly converted to tree-covered areas (51% of the total) and artificial surfaces, such as buildings and roads (37% of the total) (Figure 1.2), while 49% of the grassland lost was converted to sparse vegetation areas and 28% to tree-covered areas (Figure 1.3). There are regional variations in land conversion: in European OECD countries, where croplands and grasslands were mainly converted to tree-covered areas, while in the Asian and Oceanian OECD countries, cropland conversion was dominated by artificial surfaces and grassland by sparse vegetation. In most OECD countries, the decline in agricultural land has not affected agriculture production, which has continued to increase.

Conversion of permanent pastureland drove most of the changes in the use of agricultural land in OECD countries during the 2002-14 period. In Chile, Estonia, Greece, Luxembourg and the United States, the expansion of permanent pasture explains most of the changes in these countries, while in countries such as Austria, Iceland and New Zealand, which saw sharp declines in agricultural land, permanent pasture shrank faster than arable land and permanent cropland.

Pesticide sales in OECD countries averaged 0.93 kg/ha in the 2011-15 period (Figure 1.4I). n countries such as Italy, Portugal and Spain, which have relatively large pesticide sales per unit of land, permanent cropland makes up nearly 20% of all agricultural land, a share four times the average of OECD countries as a whole. Permanent cropland is planted with permanent crops such as fruit and berry trees, bushes, vines and olive trees. In countries with low levels of pesticide use per unit of land such as Australia, Iceland and Ireland, pasture makes up more than 80% of agricultural land, which is twice the average share in OECD countries.

Fungicides are the most widely used pesticides in OECD countries (37% of all pesticides), followed by herbicides (32%) and insecticides (13%) (Figure 1.5). In Italy, Portugal and Slovenia, fungicides account for more than 60% of total pesticide sales, while in Australia, Canada, Denmark, Estonia, Finland, Iceland, Ireland, Latvia, Lithuania, Norway, Sweden and the United States, herbicides represent at least 60% of all pesticides sold. The type of pesticide used is associated with the level of usage per unit of land (using sales as a proxy for use). In countries where use is high (pesticide sales per hectare), fungicides also make up a large share of total pesticide sales, while in countries where the use of pesticide per hectare is low, the share of herbicides tends to be high. In European countries, fungicide use is closely associated with the cultivation of grapes (EUROSTAT, 2007[23]).

Figure 1.1. Agricultural land area is decreasing in the majority of OECD countries

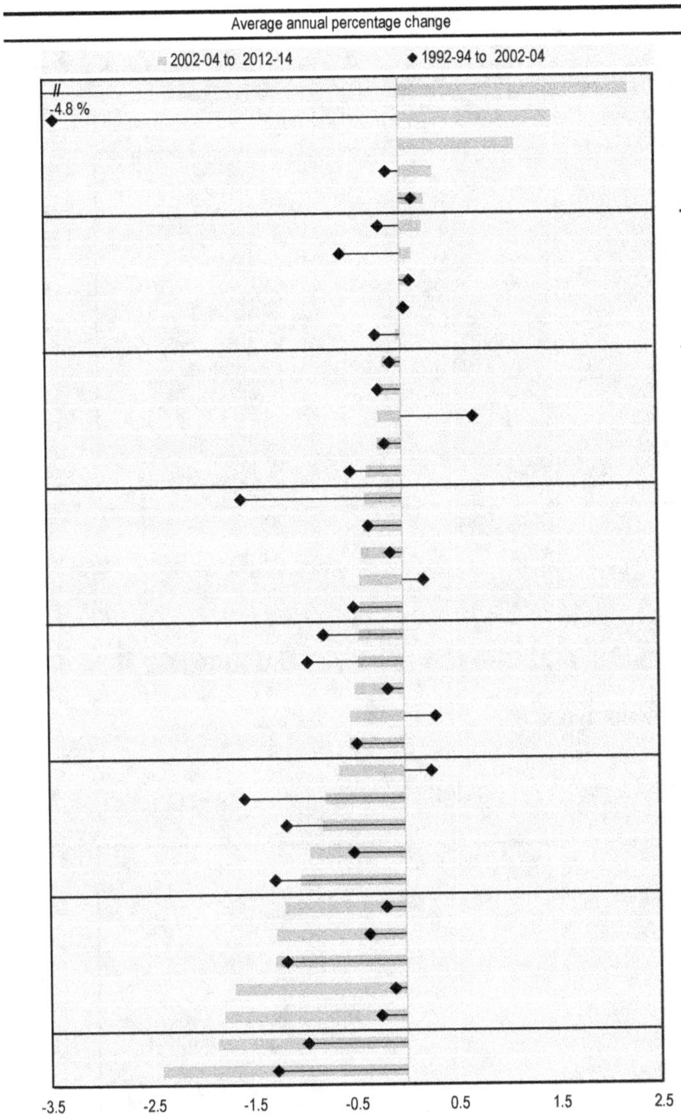

	Average (thousand hectares)		
	1992-94	2002-04	2012-14
Estonia	1 265	773	966
Latvia	2 270	1 606	1 864
Greece	n.a.	4 784	5 350
Ireland	4 405	4 349	4 492
Luxembourg	127	128	131
United States	423 172	414 631	423 568
Finland	2 380	2 245	2 270
Chile	15 494	15 642	15 766
Mexico	106 182	106 557	106 705
Denmark	2 726	2 660	2 648
Germany	17 175	17 001	16 697
Switzerland	1 591	1 556	1 526
United Kingdom	16 461	17 650	17 260
France	30 130	29 644	28 969
Sweden	3 303	3 141	3 035
Czech Republic	4 282	3 651	3 521
OECD	1 306 346	1 269 107	1 222 923
Canada	61 772	61 050	58 661
Belgium	1 365	1 393	1 335
Portugal	4 044	3 854	3 694
Japan	5 124	4 738	4 535
Slovenia	552	502	480
Netherlands	1 964	1 934	1 843
Norway	1 011	1 042	989
EU15	134 023	127 954	121 263
Turkey	39 971	41 017	38 460
Spain	29 784	25 422	23 510
Korea	2 129	1 895	1 748
Australia	465 033	442 216	402 786
Slovak Republic	2 429	2 136	1 927
Hungary	6 129	6 016	5 341
New Zealand	13 089	12 632	11 122
Poland	18 487	16 443	14 455
Iceland	1 906	1 885	1 591
Austria	3 455	3 372	2 814
Italy	16 704	15 161	12 565
Israel	435	383	300

Average annual percentage change — ▪ 2002-04 to 2012-14 — ◆ 1992-94 to 2002-04

Notes: Countries are ranked in descending order according to the average annual growth rate between 2002-04 and 2012-14. Agricultural land is defined as arable and permanent cropland plus permanent and temporary pasture.

Source: (OECD, 2018[24]).

Figure 1.2. Cropland conversion to tree cover and artificial surfaces in OECD countries

Share of cropland area in 2004 converted to other land cover types in 2015 (%)

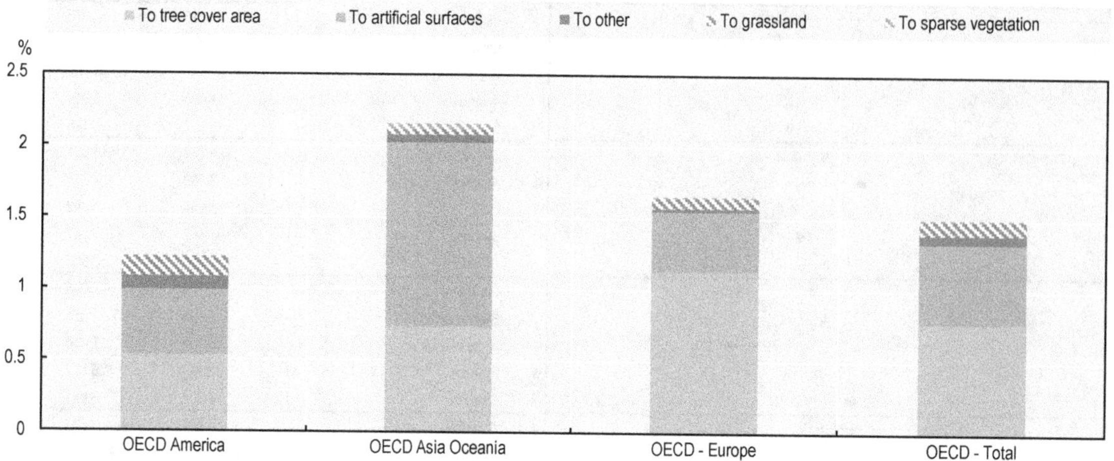

Source: (OECD, 2018[25]).

Figure 1.3. Grassland conversion to sparse vegetation and tree cover in OECD countries, 2015

Share of grassland area in 2004 converted to other land cover types (%)

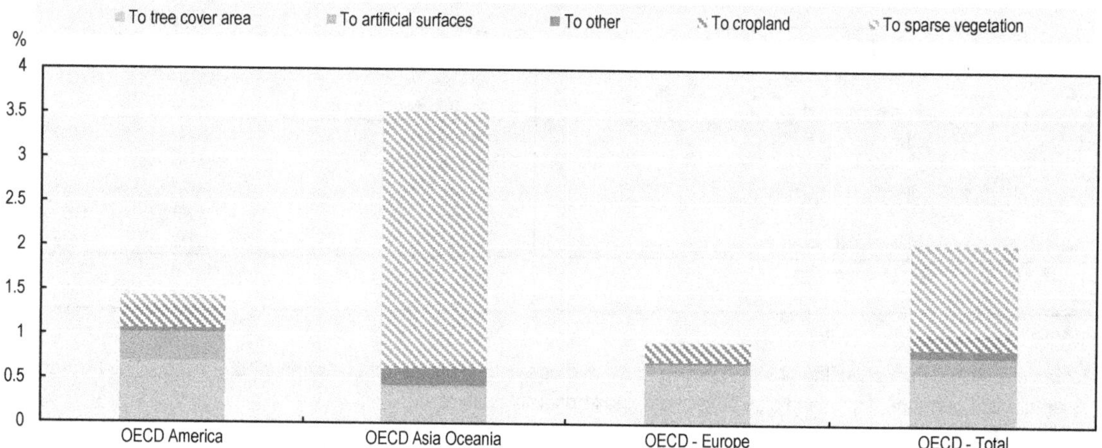

Source: (OECD, 2018[25]).

Figure 1.4. Pesticide sales per unit of land vary significantly across OECD countries, 2011-15

Average annual pesticides sales (kg/ha)		Pesticide sales (tonnes)	Agricultural land (1000 ha)
	Israel [1]	6 046	293
	Japan	53 404	4 532
	Korea	18 909	1 739
	Netherlands	10 738	1 846
	Belgium	6 490	1 335
	Italy	60 748	12 605
	Portugal	11 897	3 686
	Spain	72 818	23 664
	Germany	45 560	16 709
	Chile [2, 4]	42 316	15 772
	France	66 798	28 975
	Slovenia	1 022	475
	Czech Republic	6 016	3 512
	Hungary	8 588	5 342
	Poland	22 678	14 508
	Denmark	4 008	2 650
	Switzerland	2 192	1 526
	Canada	72 881	58 605
	Austria	3 451	2 806
	United Kingdom	21 050	17 220
	Greece	5 862	5 324
	Slovak Republic	2 056	1 926
	Turkey	40 066	38 432
	Mexico [2]	107 440	106 705
	Luxembourg	132	131
	United States	403 932	420 040
	OECD [3]	1 007 980	1 082 910
	Lithuania	2 487	2 900
	Sweden	2 353	3 039
	Norway	746	986
	Latvia	1 307	1 858
	Finland	1 591	2 273
	Ireland	3 140	4 492
	Estonia	557	967
	Australia	48 455	396 920
	Iceland	3	1 591

0   5   10   15   20   25 %

Notes

1. For Israel, 2013-15 was replaced by 2011-13.

2. For Chile and Mexico, pesticides sales are not in active ingredients.

3. The OECD total does not include Chile and Mexico as units are not in active ingredients.

4. Agricultural land area data for Chile are not official and were obtained from FAO (2018[26]).

Source: (OECD, 2018[24]).

Figure 1.5. Share of fungicides and herbicides sold in OECD countries, 2011-15

Average % of pesticides sales (active or chemical ingredients) by type

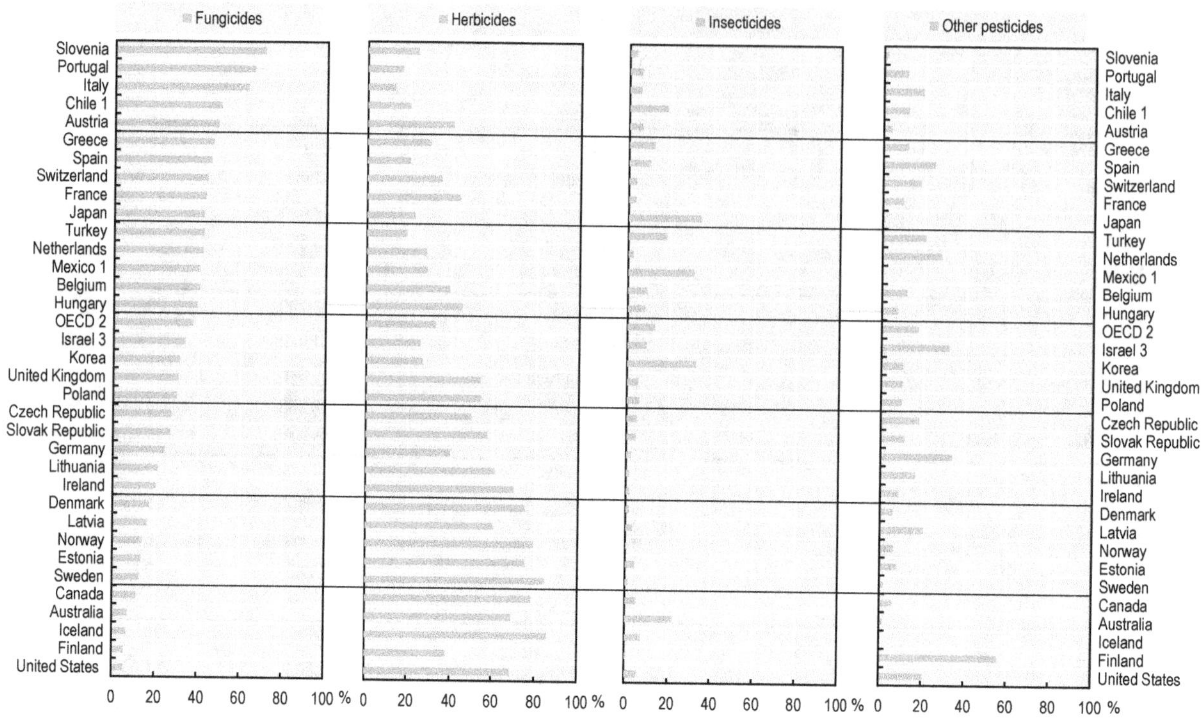

Notes: Countries are ranked in descending order of average fungicide share.
1. For Chile and Mexico, pesticide sales are not in active ingredients.
2. OECD does not include Chile and Mexico as units are not in active ingredients.
3. For Israel, 2011-15 is replaced by 2013-15.
Source: (OECD, 2018[24]).

Declining population of farmland birds in OECD countries

The indicator of farmland birds continued to decline in the period 2002-14 in almost all OECD countries where it is monitored (Figure 1.6). The exceptions were Switzerland, which reversed a decline in the farmland bird indicator for the period 1992-2004, and Latvia, where the slightly positive trends observed during the period 1992-2004 increased in the 2002-14 period. Some countries, such as Belgium, Canada, Denmark and France, were able to slow the rate of decline. In other countries, such as the Czech Republic, Estonia, Finland, Netherlands, Norway and Sweden, the rate of decline was more pronounced during the period 2002-14.

Figure 1.6. Farmland bird indicators continued to decline in most OECD countries

Average annual % change in farmland bird index (2000=100)

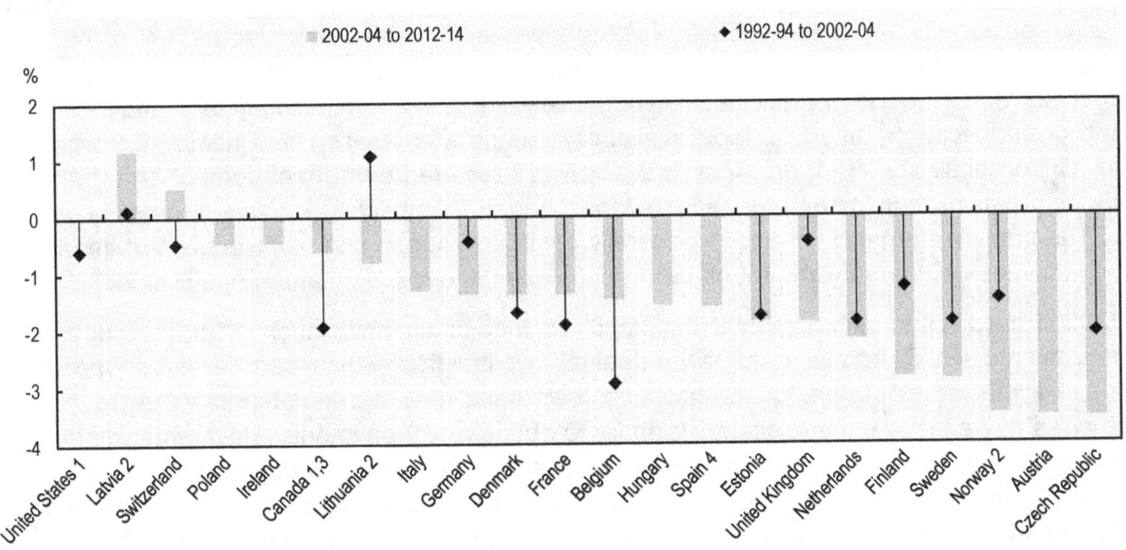

Notes: The farmland bird index is an aggregated index of population trend estimates of a selected group of breeding bird species that are dependent on agricultural land for nesting or breeding. Countries are ranked in descending order according to average percentage change 2002-04 to 2012-14.
1. For Canada and the United States, these are only grassland breeding birds.
2. For Latvia, Lithuania and Norway, 1992-94 is replaced by 1995-1997.
3. For Canada, 2012-14 is replaced by 2008-10.
4. For Spain, 2012-14 is replaced by 2006-08.
Source: (OECD, 2018[24]).

The impact of agricultural intensification and agri-environmental policies on farmland birds

While agricultural intensification has resulted in increasing yields and has sustained food production for a growing population, it has also adversely affected biodiversity, particularly the population of farmland birds (Landis, 2017[1]; Donald, Green and Heath, 2001[4]; Donald et al., 2006[5]; Stanton, Morrissey and Clark, 2018[6]; Chamberlain et al., 2000[7]). Agricultural intensification can be broadly defined as a process that increases agricultural input use per hectare of land, usually leading to an increase in the level of production per unit of land, livestock unit and agricultural working unit (European Commission, 1999[27]). It comes in the form of increased chemical inputs and use of machinery, as well as the simplification of the agricultural landscape expressed as homogeneous land cover types and larger parcel sizes within the landscape (Firbank et al., 2008[16]). Agricultural activities affect farmland birds in diverse and often interconnected ways (Chamberlain et al., 2000[7]): it reduces their food supplies; provides less suitable nesting habitats; and increases direct mortality caused by farming operations. Declines in bird populations could be the result of reduced breeding productivity or reduced survival outside the breeding season. Such declines are usually observed with some lag following agricultural intensification (Chamberlain et al., 2000[7]).

OECD countries have adopted several policy instruments to counter the environmental impact of agriculture intensification. One such instrument is the use of agri-environmental payments – voluntary programmes that offer monetary incentives to farmers to implement environmentally-friendly farming measures that go beyond those required by regulations (OECD, 2010[28]). These policies promote a wide range of practices, such as reduced chemical inputs, crop rotation, enhancement and improvement of habitats for wildlife, land retirement and conversion, buffer strips, field margins, and conservation of genetic resources (Science for Environment Policy, 2017[29]).

Agricultural practices that increase the ecological quality of uncultivated areas and that optimise and minimise the use of pesticides can be particularly beneficial for farmland biodiversity. Management and preservation of uncultivated areas such as field margins and buffers, grassland strips or patches can provide forage and nesting benefits for farmland birds (Stanton, Morrissey and Clark, 2018[6]; Aebischer et al., 2016[30]). Since the use of pesticides can negatively impact the population of farmland birds via direct poisoning or, indirectly, by affecting food availability (seeds and insects) and habitat for breeding and foraging (Chiron et al., 2014[31]), practices that support integrated pest management and that minimise pesticide applications can potentially reduce those negative impacts (Stanton, Morrissey and Clark, 2018[6]). The impact of organic farming is generally positive in supporting biodiversity, but the magnitude of the impact varies with organism groups (arthropods, plants, birds, etc.) and crop (Tuck et al., 2014[32]).

The OECD monitors agri-environmental payments by measuring how much of the average Producer Support Estimate (PSE) comes with environmental constraints,[2] which can be either mandatory or voluntary. Payments conditional on compliance with basic environmental practices are considered mandatory as these are a prerequisite for farmers to obtain direct payments. Payments with mandatory environmental constraints are also called "cross-compliance". Payments requiring specific practices going beyond basic requirements are voluntary as they are not a prerequisite for accessing direct payments. The latter include agri-environmental payments or schemes. The percentage of total PSE which has voluntary environmental constraints differs widely across countries (Figure 1.7). Among the countries that have PSE with voluntary environmental constraints in the PSE database, Australia has the highest share (22%) followed by the United States (15%); Korea (3%) and Norway (2%) have the smallest. The distribution of support per hectare also differs widely. Over the period 2012-15, annual support with environmental constraints averaged EUR 428/ha in Japan, EUR 340/ha in Korea and EUR 285/ha in Switzerland; the lowest support was in Mexico (EUR 4/ha) and Australia (EUR 0.4/ha).[3]

Figure 1.7. Share of the Producer Support Estimate with voluntary environmental constraints in OECD countries

Average PSE with voluntary environmental constraints as % of total PSE, 2012-17

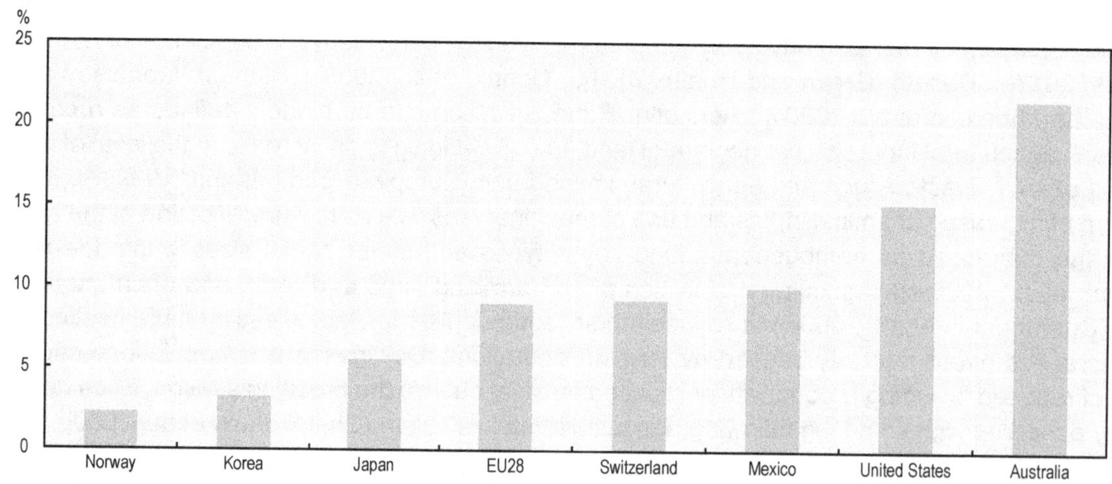

Source: (OECD, 2018[33]).

Agricultural support can be either coupled – linked to production or based on input use – or decoupled from production or input use, the latter commonly based on non-commodity criteria. Most agricultural support with voluntary environmental constraints is coupled (72%) (OECD, 2018[33]); of the remaining (28%), the majority is for long-term resource retirement (set aside) (OECD, 2018[33]). From the data available, it is possible to examine the impact of agricultural land use, the intensity of pesticide use and agri-environmental payments on farmland biodiversity by conducting an econometric analysis to test the effect on farmland bird indices of cropland, pesticide sales intensity and PSEs with environmental constraints (Annex 1.A describes the econometric model). The results presented in Table 1.1 show a negative relationship between coupled support with environmental constraints and farmland bird populations, and a positive relationship between decoupled support with environmental constraints and farmland bird indices.

The database used for the econometric regression is an unbalanced panel of 22 countries[4] over 24 years (1990-2014), which was constructed using several data sources (Annex 1.A). Using a fixed effects model to control for country characteristics, four models were estimated: Model (1) includes only land use variables (the land area used for fruits and vegetables, oil crops, cereals, and permanent pasture as a share of total agricultural area). Model (2) adds pesticide intensity of use by type (insecticides, herbicides, fungicides and bactericides and other pesticides) and nutrient balances. Model (3) includes temperature variables over four seasons: March-May, June-August, September-November and December-February. Model (4) is the most comprehensive specification, which also adds gross domestic product (GDP) per capita and PSE-related variables with environmental constraints. Based on the PSE classification, three PSE-related variables with voluntary environmental constraints were constructed: 1) coupled support with voluntary environmental constraints; 2) decoupled support with voluntary environmental constraints for the long-term retirement of factors of production; and 3) decoupled support with voluntary environmental constraints for the use of farm resources to produce specific non-commodity outputs of goods and services.[5] While voluntary environmental constraints can lower the environmental impact of coupled support, they may not be as effective at improving environmental conditions as decoupled agri-environmental payments.

The findings show that an increase of 10% in coupled support with environmental constraints is associated with a 1% *reduction* in the farmland bird index (Table 1.1). A similar increase in decoupled support with environmental constraints on the use of farm resources to produce specific non-commodity outputs of goods and services is associated with a 6% *increase* in the farmland bird index. The coefficient of decoupled support with voluntary environmental constraints for the long-term retirement of factors of production is positive, but it is not statistically significant. Comprehensive reviews of the impact of agri-environmental schemes support these results and show that decoupled payments are more effective at improving biodiversity than coupled payments related to production (Batáry et al., 2015[34]; OECD, 2018[35]). While this evidence draws mostly from farm-level studies in specific regions within a given country, policies that promote land sparing (long-retirement) in one country can have unintended consequences. The reason is that such policies can decrease yields and production in the country in which they are adopted, which can stimulate land conversion to agricultural uses and higher production in other countries, potentially affecting areas with high biodiversity (Green et al., 2005[36]; Fischer et al., 2008[37]; Balmford, Green and Phalan, 2012[38]).

Additional results show that the farmland bird index is positively associated with oil crops. A 10% increase in land under oil crops as a share of total agricultural land is associated with a 0.6% increase in the farmland bird index (Table 1.1). The main oilseed crops produced in OECD countries are soybeans, rapeseed (canola), and sunflower. Rape crops can provide feeding and nesting resources for a range of farmland bird species (OECD, 2004[39]) and have been shown to be positively associated with farmland bird populations (Green, Osborne and Sears, 1994[40]), but less suitable for bird nesting and breeding than other types of crops, such as sugar beet (Glemnitz, Zander and Stachow, 2015[41]).

Table 1.1. Farmland birds may benefit from decoupled agricultural support with environmental constraints

	(1)	(2)	(3)	(4)
Share of fruits and vegetables in total agricultural land	-0.069	-0.085	-0.086	-0.086
	[(0.063)]	[(0.062)]	[(0.060)]	[(0.059)]
Share of oil crops in total agricultural land	0.053***	0.068***	0.065***	0.059***
	[(0.017)]	[(0.016)]	[(0.015)]	[(0.015)]
Share of cereals in total agricultural land	0.055	0.021	0.026	0.107
	[(0.088)]	[(0.115)]	[(0.114)]	[(0.096)]
Share of permanent pasture in total agricultural land	-0.037	-0.086	-0.076	-0.037
	[(0.027)]	[(0.060)]	[(0.060)]	[(0.058)]
Insecticides per hectare		-0.036*	-0.034*	-0.042**
		[(0.018)]	[(0.018)]	[(0.018)]
Herbicides per hectare		0.040	0.044	0.034
		[(0.032)]	[(0.032)]	[(0.030)]
Other pesticides per hectare		-0.009	-0.013	-0.005
		[(0.017)]	[(0.017)]	[(0.016)]
Fungicides per hectare		0.027	0.027	0.022
		[(0.017)]	[(0.017)]	[(0.018)]
GDP per capita				0.063
				[(0.122)]
Coupled support per hectare				-0.107***
				[0.027]
Decoupled support per hectare: long-term resource retirement				0.104
				[0.16]
Decoupled support per hectare: specific non-commodity output				0.602***
				[0.178]
Temperature Mar-May			-0.001	-0.0005
			[0.0012]	[0.001]
Temperature Jun-Aug			-0.004**	-0.004**
			[0.002]	[0.001]
Temperature Sep-Nov			-0.002*	-0.001
			[0.001]	[0.001]
Temperature Dec-Feb			0.0005	0.0003
			[0.001]	[0.001]
Nitrogen balance per hectare		-0.00001	9.80E-06	-9.25E-06
		[0.0001]	[0.0001]	[0.0001]
Phosphorus balance per hectare		0.0003	0.0003	0.0003
		[0.0007]	[0.0007]	[0.0006]
Constant	16.939***	17.193***	14.746**	32.012***
	[(2.640)]	[(5.789)]	[(5.859)]	[(8.865)]
Observations	453	404	404	404
R-squared	0.631	0.662	0.670	0.687

Notes: Coefficients were estimated using a fixed-effect model and robust standard errors are presented in parenthesis. The dependent variable is the logged value of the farmland birds index. Coefficients are expressed in elasticities. The PSE variables reflect nationally funded measures, which means that for EU countries EU-funded measures are excluded.

*, ** and *** represent statistically significant coefficients at the 10%, 5% and 1% levels, respectively. All models include year dummies and a trend. The sample covers 1990-2014 for 22 countries.

Sources: Data for pesticides were obtained from FAOSTAT (2018[26]); land use data were extracted from FAOSTAT (2018[26]) and OECD AEIs (2018[24]); GDP per capita data were obtained from World Bank Development Indicators Database (2018[42]); PSE variables were constructed from PSE database (OECD, 2018[33]) and temperature data were obtained from the Climatic Research Unit (2019[43]). Nutrient balances were obtained from OECD AEIs (2018[24]).

In general, farmland bird diversity and density tend to be lower on maize-cultivated lands (Jerrentrup et al., 2017[18]; Turley, 2006[19]). In the empirical analysis performed, the share of pasture area was not statistically significant, but several studies have reported the importance of pasture for bird diversity (Cerezo, Conde and Poggio, 2011[44]; Hartel et al., 2014[45]). Additional factors that improve the diversity of bird species are landscape heterogeneity, represented by a combination of crop fields and perennial features such as trees, bushes and other woody elements (Redlich et al., 2018[46]; Pickett and Siriwardena, 2011[47]; Cerezo, Conde and Poggio, 2011[44]), and small fields (Zellweger-Fischer et al., 2018[48]). There can be differences between low-ranging and wide-ranging species, with the former preferring more homogeneous landscapes (Katayama et al., 2014[49]).

Warmer temperatures in the summer negatively affect farmland bird indices. A 10% increase in summer temperatures reduces the index by 0.04% (Table 1.1). This finding is in line with research results that point to the impact of long-term climate trends on abundance and richness of bird species (Stephens et al., 2016[50]; Pearce-Higgins et al., 2015[51]; Both et al., 2006[52]). One way climate change affects bird populations is that organisms at a lower position in the food chain (e.g. insects, flowering plants) are adapting to a hotter climate by bringing forward their seasonal activities, while birds are responding at a slower pace to a changing climate, generating misalignments between breeding time and food supply abundance (Both et al., 2006[52]).

The use of pesticides is considered a key driver in the decline farmland bird populations (Stanton, Morrissey and Clark, 2018[6]; OECD, 2018[15]). Pesticides can directly impact birds by poisoning or indirectly by affecting habitat and disrupting food web chains due to the removal of insect and seed food sources (BirdLife International, 2015[53]). The results of the econometric exercise show that a 10% increase in insecticide intensity (sales per hectare) is associated with a 0.4% decline in the farmland bird index (Table 1.1). Of particular concern for invertebrates such as pollinator colonies, as well as for insectivorous birds, is the application of certain neonicotinoid insecticides (Hallmann et al., 2014[54]; Gill, Ramos-Rodriguez and Raine, 2012[55]). Since 2013, the European Union has severely restricted the use of three neonicotinoids (*clothianidin*, *imidacloprid* and *thiamethoxam*) due to their potentially negative impact on bee populations (European Food Safety Authority, 2018[56]). Some OECD countries – such as Denmark, France, Italy, Mexico, Norway and Sweden – have implemented pesticide taxes to reduce pesticide risks (OECD, 2018[15]). While instruments targeted at single substances can reduce risks in the short-term, a proper evaluation of the unintended effects from these instruments, such as induced land use changes and potentially increased application rates of substitute substances, should be properly accounted for.

1.3. Policy responses by Switzerland to a declining farmland bird population

The Swiss farmland bird index, composed of 38 bird species commonly found on farmland, has remained stable since 2000. However, the Environmental Objectives of Agriculture (EOA) targeted species index that focuses on targeted farmland bird species tells a less favourable story (Figure 1.8). The EOA index was created following the publication of the Environmental Targets for Agriculture in 2008 by the Swiss Federal Office for the Environment and the Federal Office for Agriculture (updated in 2016) (OECD, 2017[57]). The Environmental Targets for Agriculture set specific goals related to thematic areas, including biodiversity and landscape, climate and air, water, and soil (OECD, 2017[57]). It prompted a revision of the farmland birds indicator; a more accurate methodology and definition of species to render the indicator more sensitive to policy changes and more linked to specific environmental goals was implemented.

The Environmental Targets for Agriculture policy imposed specific targets for conserving and favouring indigenous species. In accordance with these objectives, the Swiss Ornithological Institute defined two lists of species: "targeted" and "characteristic". The EOA target species index is composed of 28 species, all facing different degrees of risk according to national assessments, and are further classified as critically endangered, endangered, vulnerable, or near threatened. Currently, four species (10% of the total list) are critically endangered. The EOA characteristics species index is composed of 17 species commonly found in specific habitats, such as hedgerows. In contrast to species in the EOA index, characteristic species have been relatively stable since 1990 (Figure 1.8).

One of the most important agri-environmental measures for biodiversity conservation in Switzerland has been the creation of Biodiversity Promotion Areas (BPAs), previously called Ecological Compensation Areas.[6] The objective of the BPAs is to create habitats for plants and wildlife. In order for farmers to be eligible for direct payments, they need to set aside 7% of their agricultural land as BPAs. Farmers can decide among 16 options for these areas with varying ecological qualities, including wildflower strips, meadows, extensively used pasture, hedgerows, and other traditional farmland habitat. In addition, input use in BPAs is constrained; in particular, fertiliser use is prohibited, chemical controls and mulching are not allowed, and grass must be cut and discharged at specific dates. Farmers can claim additional quality-based payments for BPAs on which plants of particularly high ecological relevance grow (QII BPAs). To be eligible for QII BPA payments, in addition to fulfilling the aforementioned input constraints, the area subject for payment must prove its botanical quality or have specific structures for the promotion of biodiversity.

Figure 1.8. Trends in farmland bird populations in selected European countries, 1990-2016

Farmland bird index (1990=100)

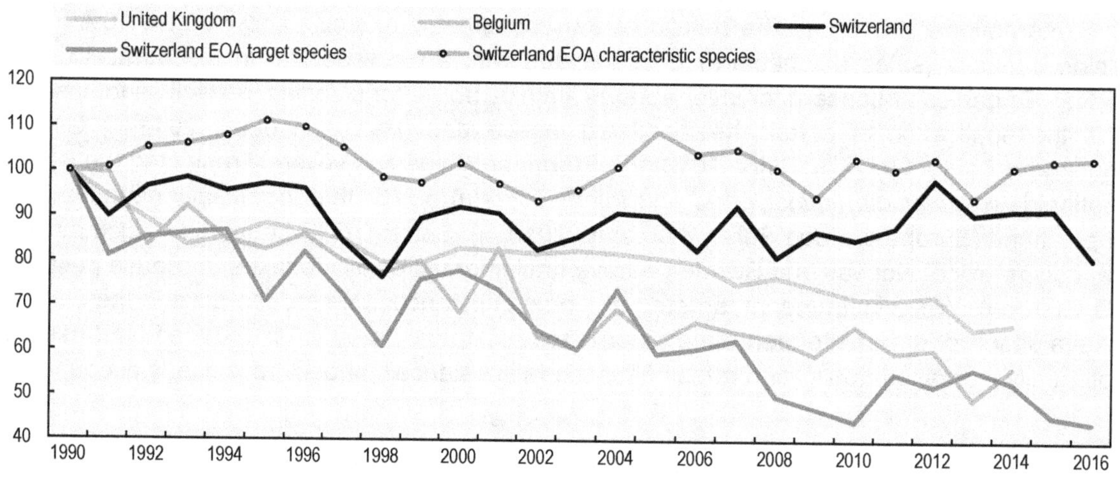

Sources: Indices for the United Kingdom, Belgium, and Switzerland were obtained from (OECD, 2018[24]). Switzerland EOA indices were obtained from Swiss Bird Index®, https://www.vogelwarte.ch/en/projects/population-trends/sbi-state/.

Overall, BPAs have had a moderate effect on supporting farmland bird populations at the landscape level (Birrer et al., 2007[58]; Herzog et al., 2005[59]). Generally, they have improved bird populations that are not at risk but they have not been successful at halting the decline of at-risk and targeted species. A frequently cited reason for the limited effectiveness of this measure is that most BPAs are of relatively low ecological quality (Birrer et al., 2007[58]). Evidence shows that BPAs tend to be successful at supporting biodiversity when the areas are of high ecological quality, such as wildflower strips or high ecological quality meadows (Meichtry-Stier et al., 2014[60]) and when they are established in ecologically suitable areas. When evaluated at the landscape level, the richness of birds and butterflies species tends to decrease with fewer BPA areas (Zingg, Grenz and Humbert, 2018[61]).

Subsequent agricultural reforms over the past two decades made the preservation, conservation and promotion of biodiversity a key objective. As a consequence, direct payments to livestock farmers were removed and farmers received increased payments for meeting biodiversity goals such as devoting larger areas to extensive upland grazing, building ecological networks and increasing the share of high-quality BPAs. In 2002, high-quality BPAs accounted for 1% of total agricultural land and 11% of total BPAs. By 2017, this had increased to 6.3% of agricultural land and 40% of total BPAs. Since 2015, following the latest reform of agricultural policies, high-quality BPAs increased by 20% and Switzerland became one of the OECD countries that spends more on agri-environmental payments per hectare (PSE support with environmental constraints) relative to other OECD countries (Figure 1.10). More importantly, nearly 90% of Switzerland's support with environmental constraints is now decoupled from production.

To improve biodiversity, the government has also promoted the establishment of ecological networks by linking biodiverse areas. Farmers participating in BPAs can receive additional payments if they belong to a regional network of BPAs, which has to be developed and operated according to the guidelines of a regional networking project approved by a canton (local government). A networking project lasts eight years. As of 2017, 75% of BPAs belonged to a network.

While it is too early to evaluate the environmental impact of the reforms on agricultural policies, including those of 2014, they have improved the targeting and decoupling of support for farmers which, in turn, could have a positive impact on biodiversity in the medium and long term. The decline of at-risk species still represents a key challenge in Switzerland, however. Increasing the geographical coverage of high-quality BPAs could help to improve biodiversity in Swiss farmland. To completely reverse the negative trends observed for some species, and considering that other factors such as land-use change, climate change and crop mix, impact farmland bird populations, Switzerland needs to increase its efforts. It is estimated that high-quality BPAs should make up 14% of total farmland to recover farmland bird populations (Meichtry-Stier et al., 2014[60]), particularly those at risk. At the same time, it is important to evaluate the potential impacts on yields and productivity of policies that aim to improve biodiversity on farmland so as to minimise their unintended effects, such as the clearance of remote and highly valuable ecosystems for agriculture (Green et al., 2005[36]; Fischer et al., 2008[37]; Balmford, Green and Phalan, 2012[38]).

Figure 1.9. High quality Biodiversity Promotion Areas (BPAs) have increased but represent a low share in total agricultural land

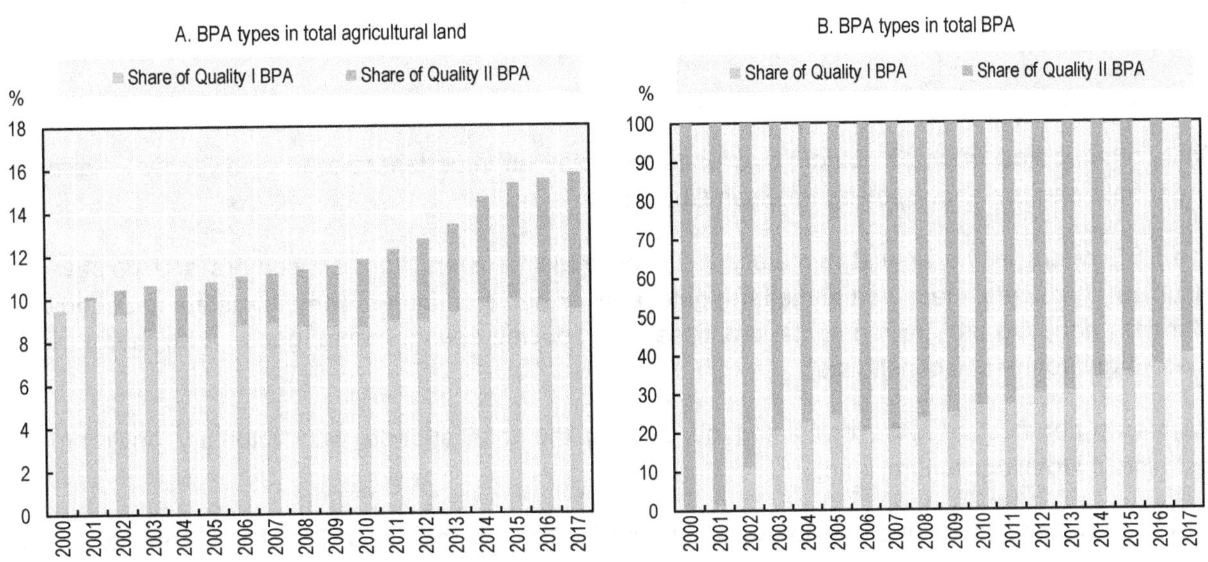

Note: Total agricultural land is total utilized agricultural area and does not include summer pasture.
Source: Swiss Federal Office of Agriculture (FOAG).

Figure 1.10. Agri-environmental payments increased sharply in Switzerland

PSE with environmental constraints (EUR/ha)

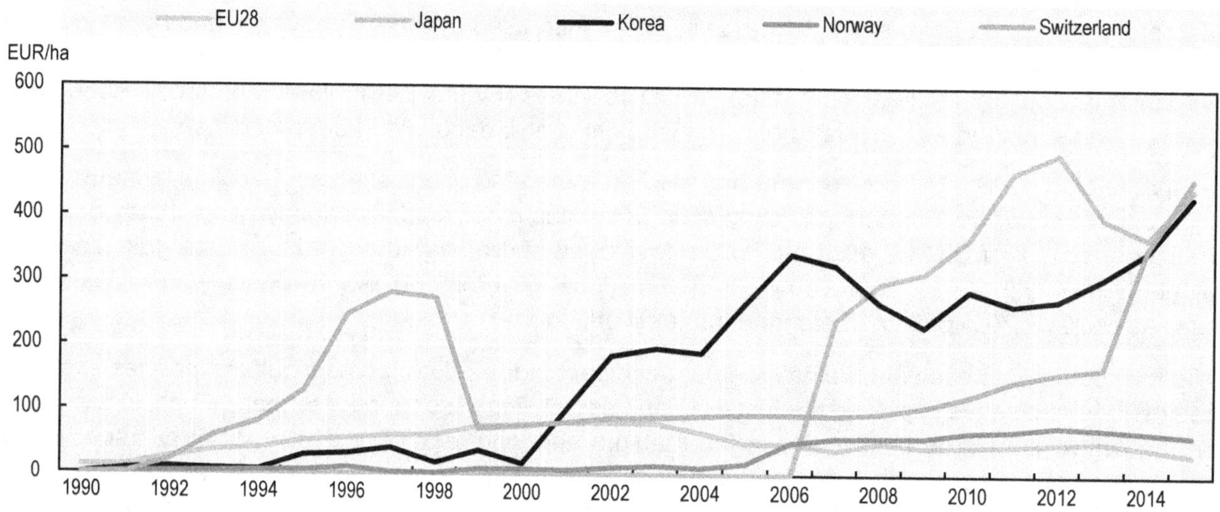

Sources: PSE data were obtained from the OECD Producer and Consumer Support Estimates database (OECD, 2018[33]), while land use data were retrieved from the OECD Agri-environmental Indicators database (OECD, 2018[24]).

Notes

[1] While other factors such as nutrient surpluses may play an important role on biodiversity in farmland, nutrient balances are analysed separately in Chapter 3.

[2] The PSE refers to the annual monetary value of gross transfers from consumers and taxpayers to agricultural producers, measured at the farm gate level. In some countries, some transfers are conditional on farmers adopting pro-environmental practices or producing environmental goods and, therefore, are subject to environmental constraints.

[3] Payments per hectare were calculated by dividing the total support with voluntary environmental constraints by total agricultural land.

[4] Farmland bird indices are available for Austria, Belgium, Canada, the Czech Republic, Denmark, Estonia, Finland, France, Germany, Hungary, Ireland, Italy, Latvia, Lithuania, the Netherlands, Norway, Poland, Spain, Sweden, Switzerland, the United Kingdom and the United States. For the United States and Canada, the data series are incomplete.

[5] Support to agriculture in the European Union is either entirely financed by the European Union or co-financed by the European Union and member countries. It was not possible to recover all national-level PSE with environmental constraints measures from the underlying databases for constructing the EU PSE, mainly because the EU-funded share is not available by country for the years before 2012. Another drawback of the EU-funded share is that, for the period that is available, it is not divided by type of support (coupled or decoupled). Hence, for EU countries the PSE variables with environmental constraints mainly represent the nationally funded shares of PSE with environmental constraints. Robustness checks of the econometric exercise included adding the EU-funded share; results of such exercise indicate that coupled support is negative and statistically significant although the number of observations sharply decrease.

[6] The term Ecological Compensation Area was changed to Biodiversity Promotion Area in the 2014-17 agriculture reform.

References

Aebischer, N. et al. (2016), "Twenty years of local farmland bird conservation: The effects of management on avian abundance at two UK demonstration sites", *Bird Study*, Vol. 63/1, http://dx.doi.org/10.1080/00063657.2015.1090391. [30]

Balmford, A., R. Green and B. Phalan (2012), "What conservationists need to know about farming", *Proceedings of the Royal Society B: Biological Sciences*, http://dx.doi.org/10.1098/rspb.2012.0515. [38]

Bartomeus, I. et al. (2013), "Historical changes in northeastern US bee pollinators related to shared ecological traits", *Proceedings of the National Academy of Sciences*, http://dx.doi.org/10.1073/pnas.1218503110. [9]

Batáry, P. et al. (2015), "The role of agri-environment schemes in conservation and environmental management.", *Conservation biology*, Vol. 29/4, pp. 1006-16, http://dx.doi.org/10.1111/cobi.12536. [34]

BirdLife International (2015), *BirdLife Europe position paper: reducing direct and indirect impacts of pesticides on birds*, https://www.birdlife.org/sites/default/files/attachments/20150504_ATF-pesticides-position.pdf. [53]

Birrer, S. et al. (2007), "The Swiss agri-environment scheme promotes farmland birds: but only moderately", *Journal of Ornithology*, Vol. 148/S2, pp. 295-303, http://dx.doi.org/10.1007/s10336-007-0237-y. [58]

Both, C. et al. (2006), "Climate change and population declines in a long-distance migratory bird", *Nature*, Vol. 441, pp. 81-83, http://dx.doi.org/10.1038/nature04539. [52]

Cerezo, A., M. Conde and S. Poggio (2011), "Pasture area and landscape heterogeneity are key determinants of bird diversity in intensively managed farmland", *Biodiversity Conservation*, Vol. 20, pp. 2649-2667, http://dx.doi.org/10.1007/s10531-011-0096-y. [44]

Chamberlain, D. et al. (2000), "Changes in the abundance of farmland birds in relation to the timing of agricultural intensification in England and Wales", *Journal of Applied Ecology*, Vol. 37/5, pp. 771-788, http://dx.doi.org/10.1046/j.1365-2664.2000.00548.x. [7]

Chiron, F. et al. (2014), "Pesticide doses, landscape structure and their relative effects on farmland birds", *Agriculture, Ecosystems and Environment*, Vol. 185/1, pp. 153-160, http://dx.doi.org/10.1016/j.agee.2013.12.013.   [31]

Climatic Research Unit (2019), *High-resolution gridded datasets (and derived products)*, https://crudata.uea.ac.uk/cru/data/hrg/.   [43]

de Ruiter, P. and G. Brown (2007), "Soil biodiversity for agricultural sustainability", *Agriculture, Ecosystems & Environment*, Vol. 121/3, pp. 233-244, http://dx.doi.org/10.1016/J.AGEE.2006.12.013.   [14]

Díaz, S. et al. (2006), *Biodiversity Regulation of Ecosystem Services*, Island Press.   [11]

Donald, P., R. Green and M. Heath (2001), "Agricultural intensification and the collapse of Europe's farmland bird populations", *Proceedings of the Royal Society B: Biological Sciences*, Vol. 268/1462, pp. 25–29., http://dx.doi.org/10.1098/rspb.2000.1325.   [4]

Donald, P. et al. (2006), "Further evidence of continent-wide impacts of agricultural intensification on European farmland birds, 1990-2000", *Agriculture, Ecosystems and Environment*, Vol. 116/3-4, pp. 189-196, http://dx.doi.org/10.1016/j.agee.2006.02.007.   [5]

European Birds Census Council (n.d.), *What is Pan-European Common Bird Monitoring Scheme?*, https://www.ebcc.info/pan-european-common-bird-monitoring-scheme-pecbms/what-is-pan-european-common-bird-monitoring-scheme/.   [64]

European Commission (1999), *Agriculture, Environment, Rural Development: Facts and Figures - A Challenge for Agriculture*, European Commission.   [27]

European Food Safety Authority (2018), *Neonicotinoids: Risks to bees confirmed*, European Food Safety Authority, https://www.efsa.europa.eu/en/press/news/180228.   [56]

EUROSTAT (2007), *The use of plant protection products in the European Union*, European Union.   [23]

FAOSTAT (2018), *Food and agriculture data*, http://www.fao.org/faostat/en/#home.   [26]

Firbank, L. et al. (2008), "Assessing the impacts of agricultural intensification on biodiversity: A British perspective", *Philosophical Transactions of the Royal Society B*, Vol. 363/1492, http://dx.doi.org/10.1098/rstb.2007.2183.   [16]

Fischer, J. et al. (2008), "Should agricultural policies encourage land sparing or wildlife-friendly farming?", *Frontiers in Ecology and the Environment*, Vol. 6/7, pp. 380-385, http://dx.doi.org/10.1890/070019.   [37]

Foley, J. et al. (2011), "Solutions for a cultivated planet", *Nature*, Vol. 478, pp. 337–342, http://dx.doi.org/10.1038/nature10452.   [21]

Gill, R., O. Ramos-Rodriguez and N. Raine (2012), "Combined pesticide exposure severely affects individual- and colony-level traits in bees", *Nature*, Vol. 491/7422, pp. 105-108, http://dx.doi.org/10.1038/nature11585.   [55]

Glemnitz, M., P. Zander and U. Stachow (2015), "Regionalizing land use impacts on farmland birds.", *Environmental monitoring and assessment*, Vol. 187/6, p. 336, http://dx.doi.org/10.1007/s10661-015-4448-z.   [41]

Green, R. et al. (2005), "Farming and the fate of wild nature", *Science*, Vol. 307/5709, pp. 550-555, http://dx.doi.org/10.1126/science.1106049. [36]

Green, R., P. Osborne and E. Sears (1994), "The Distribution of Passerine Birds in Hedgerows During the Breeding Season in Relation to Characteristics of the Hedgerow and Adjacent Farmland", *The Journal of Applied Ecology*, Vol. 31/4, p. 677, http://dx.doi.org/10.2307/2404158. [40]

Hallmann, C. et al. (2014), "Declines in insectivorous birds are associated with high neonicotinoid concentrations", *Nature*, Vol. 511/7509, pp. 341-343, http://dx.doi.org/10.1038/nature13531. [54]

Hardelin, J. and J. Lankoski (2018), "Land use and ecosystem services", *OECD Food, Agriculture and Fisheries Papers*, No. 114, OECD Publishing, Paris, https://dx.doi.org/10.1787/c7ec938e-en. [13]

Harris, I. et al. (2014), "Updated high-resolution grids of monthly climatic observations - the CRU TS3.10 Dataset", *International Journal of Climatology*, http://dx.doi.org/10.1002/joc.3711. [62]

Hartel, T. et al. (2014), "Bird communities in traditional wood-pastures with changing management in Eastern Europe", *Basic and Applied Ecology*, Vol. 15/5, pp. 385-395, http://dx.doi.org/10.1016/J.BAAE.2014.06.007. [45]

Herzog, F. et al. (2005), "Effect of ecological compensation areas on floristic and breeding bird diversity in Swiss agricultural landscapes", *Agriculture, Ecosystems & Environment*, Vol. 108/3, pp. 189-204, http://dx.doi.org/10.1016/J.AGEE.2005.02.003. [59]

Hosonuma, N. et al. (2012), "An assessment of deforestation and forest degradation drivers in developing countries", *Environmental Research Letters*, Vol. 7/4, http://dx.doi.org/10.1088/1748-9326/7/4/044009. [20]

Jerrentrup, J. et al. (2017), "Impact of recent changes in agricultural land use on farmland bird trends", *Agriculture, Ecosystems & Environment*, Vol. 239, pp. 334-341, http://dx.doi.org/10.1016/J.AGEE.2017.01.041. [18]

José-María, L. et al. (2011), "How does agricultural intensification modulate changes in plant community composition?", *Agriculture, Ecosystems and Environment*, Vol. 145/1, pp. 77-84, http://dx.doi.org/10.1016/j.agee.2010.12.020. [3]

Katayama, N. et al. (2014), "Landscape heterogeneity-biodiversity relationship: Effect of range size", *PLoS ONE*, Vol. 9/3, http://dx.doi.org/10.1007/978-981-10-5041-1_31. [49]

Kleijn, D. et al. (2012), "On the relationship between farmland biodiversity and land-use intensity in Europe", *Proceedings of the Royal Society B: Biological Sciences*, http://dx.doi.org/10.1098/rspb.2008.1509. [2]

Landis, D. (2017), "Designing agricultural landscapes for biodiversity-based ecosystem services", *Basic and Applied Ecology*, Vol. 18, pp. 1-12, http://dx.doi.org/10.1016/j.baae.2016.07.005. [1]

Mace, G., K. Norris and A. Fitter (2012), "Biodiversity and ecosystem services: A multilayered relationship", *Trends in Ecology and Evolution*, Vol. 27/1, pp. 19-26, http://dx.doi.org/10.1016/j.tree.2011.08.006. [12]

Meichtry-Stier, K. et al. (2014), "Impact of landscape improvement by agri-environment scheme options on densities of characteristic farmland bird species and brown hare (Lepus europaeus)", *Agriculture, Ecosystems & Environment*, Vol. 189, pp. 101-109, http://dx.doi.org/10.1016/J.AGEE.2014.02.038. [60]

OECD (2019), *Impacts of agricultural policies on productivity and sustainability performance in agriculture: a literature review*, COM/TAD/CA/ENV/EPOC(2019)3/FINAL. [66]

OECD (2018), *Agri-environmental indicators database*, http://www.oecd.org/agriculture/topics/agriculture-and-the-environment/. [24]

OECD (2018), *Innovation, Agricultural Productivity and Sustainability in Korea*, OECD Food and Agricultural Reviews, OECD Publishing, Paris, https://dx.doi.org/10.1787/9789264307773-en. [35]

OECD (2018), *Land cover in countries and regions*, https://stats.oecd.org/Index.aspx?DataSetCode=LAND_COVER. [25]

OECD (2018), *OECD Producer and Consumer Support Estimates database*, http://www.oecd.org/tad/agricultural-policies/producerandconsumersupportestimatesdatabase.htm. [33]

OECD (2018), *Pesticide and fertiliser trends and policies across selected OECD countries: Overview and insights*, OECD internal document. [15]

OECD (2018), *The Use of New Technologies for Agri-Environmental Indicators to Support Effective Policy Monitoring, Evaluation and Design*, http://www.oecd.org/tad/Events/OECD-Luke-Workshop.htm. [65]

OECD (2017), *The Political Economy of Biodiversity Policy Reform*, OECD Publishing, Paris, http://dx.doi.org/10.1787/9789264269545-en. [57]

OECD (2013), *OECD Compendium of Agri-environmental Indicators*, OECD Publishing, Paris, http://dx.doi.org/10.1787/9789264186217-en. [63]

OECD (2010), *Guidelines for Cost-effective Agri-environmental Policy Measures*, OECD Publishing, Paris, http://dx.doi.org/10.1787/9789264086845-en. [28]

OECD (2004), *Biomass and Agriculture: Sustainability, Markets and Policies*, OECD Publishing, Paris, https://dx.doi.org/10.1787/9789264105546-en. [39]

OECD/FAO (2018), *OECD-FAO Agricultural Outlook 2018-2027*, OECD Publishing, Paris/FAO, Rome, http://dx.doi.org/10.1787/agr_outlook-2018-en. [22]

Pearce-Higgins, J. et al. (2015), "Drivers of climate change impacts on bird communities", *Journal of Animal Ecology*, Vol. 84/4, pp. 943-954, http://dx.doi.org/10.1111/1365-2656.12364. [51]

Pickett, S. and G. Siriwardena (2011), "The relationship between multi-scale habitat heterogeneity and farmland bird abundance", *Ecography*, Vol. 34/6, pp. 955-969, http://dx.doi.org/10.1111/j.1600-0587.2011.06608.x. [47]

Potts, S. et al. (2010), "Global pollinator declines: Trends, impacts and drivers", *Trends in Ecology and Evolution*, Vol. 25/6, pp. 345-353, http://dx.doi.org/10.1016/j.tree.2010.01.007. [8]

Redlich, S. et al. (2018), "Landscape heterogeneity rather than crop diversity mediates bird diversity in agricultural landscapes", *PLOS ONE*, Vol. 13/8, p. e0200438, http://dx.doi.org/10.1371/journal.pone.0200438. [46]

Sánchez-Bayo, F. and K. Wyckhuys (2019), "Worldwide decline of the entomofauna: A review of its drivers", *Biological Conservation*, Vol. 232, pp. 8-27, http://dx.doi.org/10.1016/j.biocon.2019.01.020. [10]

Science for Environment Policy (2017), *Agri-environmental schemes: how to enhance the agriculture-environment relationship*, European Commission DG Environment, Bristol, http://dx.doi.org/10.2779/633983. [29]

Stanton, R., C. Morrissey and R. Clark (2018), "Analysis of trends and agricultural drivers of farmland bird declines in North America: A review", *Agriculture, Ecosystems and Environment*, Vol. 254/15, pp. 244-254, http://dx.doi.org/10.1016/j.agee.2017.11.028. [6]

Stephens, P. et al. (2016), "Consistent response of bird populations to climate change on two continents", *Science*, Vol. 352/6281, pp. 84-87, http://dx.doi.org/10.1126/science.aac4858. [50]

Tilman, D. et al. (2001), "Forecasting agriculturally driven global environmental change", *Science*, http://dx.doi.org/10.1126/science.1057544. [17]

Tuck, S. et al. (2014), "Land-use intensity and the effects of organic farming on biodiversity: A hierarchical meta-analysis", *Journal of Applied Ecology*, Vol. 51/3, pp. 746-755, http://dx.doi.org/10.1111/1365-2664.12219. [32]

Turley, D. (2006), *Environmental impacts of cereal and oilseed cropping and potential for biofuel production*, http://citeseerx.ist.psu.edu/viewdoc/download?doi=10.1.1.625.3369&rep=rep1&type=pdf (accessed on 13 September 2018). [19]

World Bank (2018), *World Development Indicators*, https://data.worldbank.org/indicator?tab=all. [42]

Zellweger-Fischer, J. et al. (2018), "Identifying factors that influence bird richness and abundance on farms", *Bird Study*, Vol. 65/2, pp. 161-173, http://dx.doi.org/10.1080/00063657.2018.1446903. [48]

Zingg, S., J. Grenz and J. Humbert (2018), "Landscape-scale effects of land use intensity on birds and butterflies", *Agriculture, Ecosystems and Environment*, Vol. 267, pp. 119–128, https://doi.org/10.1016/j.agee.2018.08.014. [61]

Annex 1.A. Econometric model

This annex provides details about the econometric estimation performed to produce results reported in Table 1.1. The following fixed effects model was fit:

$$\log(Bird)_{ct} = \log(FrutVeg)_{ct} + \log(OilCrop)_{ct} + \log(Cereal)_{ct} + \log(Pasture)_{ct} + \log(Insec/ha)_{ct}$$
$$+ \log(Herb/ha)_{ct} + \log(OtherPest/ha)_{ct} + \log(Fung/ha)_{ct} + \log(GDPpercap)_{ct}$$
$$+ Coupled_{ct} + Decoupled\_Long\_Ret_{ct} + Decoupled\_Non\_Comm_{ct} + \sum_{i=1}^{4} Temp_{ict}$$
$$+ NBalance_{ct} + PBalance_{ct} + C + T + PestDumm + trend + e_{ct}$$

Where variables $FrutVeg$, $OilCrop$, $Cereal$ and $Pasture$ refer to the share of fruits and vegetables, oil crops, cereals and pasture cultivated area to total cultivated area, respectively; pesticides sales are included separately by type and relative to unit of land (hectares): $\frac{Insec}{ha}$, $\frac{Herb}{ha}$, $\frac{OtherPest}{ha}$ and $\frac{Fung}{ha}$ denote insecticides, herbicides, other pesticides and fungicides, respectively. The variable $GDPpercap$ refers to per capita Gross Domestic Product. The main policy variables of interest are $Coupled$, $Decoupled\_Non\_Comm$ and $Decoupled\_Long\_Ret$. Agri-environmental support coupled with either input use or output is represented by the variable $Coupled$; decoupled forms of agri-environmental support are divided into two: based on long-term resource retirement,[1] $Decoupled\_Long\_Ret$, or based on specific non-commodity output,[2] $Decoupled\_Non\_Comm$. Four country average temperature variables ($\sum_{i=1}^{4} Temp_{ict}$) were included: March-May, June-August, September-November, and December-February. Nitrogen and phosphorus balances are represented by variables $NBalance$ and $PBalance$. Country and year dummies were also included, C and T, to control for time-invariant country-specific elements (such as geographic characteristics) and time varying shocks, such as global market swings, weather shocks, etc. A trend variable, $trend$, and a dummy ($PestDumm$) that takes a value of one for European countries after 2010 were also added. The latter controls for changes in the methodology for measuring pesticides in European countries after 2010. Table 1.A.1 presents summary statistics of the data used for the analysis.

Annex Table 1.A.1 Summary statistics

Variable	Units	Mean	Std. Dev.	Min	Max
Farmland bird index	(2000=100)	95.302	14.186	58.200	157.400
Share of fruits and vegetables in total agriculture land	%	2.749	2.764	0.182	14.202
Share of oil crops in total agriculture land	%	5.396	4.071	0.050	16.518
Share of cereals in total agriculture land	%	30.696	14.030	5.999	58.503
Share of permanent pasture in total agriculture land	%	34.256	21.172	0.586	90.331
Coupled support with environmental constraints	1 000 EUR /ha	0.021	0.032	0.000	0.254
Decoupled support per hectare: long-term resource retirement	1 000 EUR /ha	0.002	0.007	0	0.086
Decoupled support per hectare: specific non-commodity output	1 000 EUR /ha	0.005	0.014	0	0.119
N balance per hectare	Kg/ha	75.562	59.232	6.661	321.000
P balance per hectare	Kg/ha	6.066	7.306	-8.000	38.000
Temperature Mar-May	°C	7.145	4.099	-9.300	13.500
Temperature Jun-Aug	°C	16.730	2.796	10.200	24.100
Temperature Sep-Nov	°C	8.458	3.764	-3.900	16.700
Temperature Dec-Feb	°C	-0.693	5.588	-21.900	8.400
Insecticides per hectare	Kg/ha	0.155	0.235	0.001	1.014
Herbicides per hectare	Kg/ha	0.798	0.637	0.087	4.009
Other pesticides per hectare	Kg/ha	0.212	0.267	0.001	1.829

Variable	Units	Mean	Std. Dev.	Min	Max
Fungicides per hectare	Kg/ha	0.648	0.839	0.027	4.078
GDP per capita	USD/capita	38268.670	18081.230	5140.528	91617.280

Note: Total observations: 405.
Sources: Farmland bird index, pesticides and nutrient balance per hectare were obtained from the OECD Agri-environmental Indicators database (OECD, 2018[24]); share of cultivated land by crop type to total land variables were calculated from FAOSTAT (2018[26]); temperature data was obtained from the Climate Research Unit of the University of East Anglia dataset consisting of country averages at a seasonal frequency, where spatial averages are calculated using area-weighted means (Harris et al., 2014[62]).

Notes

[1] These transfers are for the long-term retirement of factors of production from commodity production.

[2] These transfers are for the use of farm resources to produce specific non-commodity outputs of goods and services, which are not required by regulations.

Annex 1.B. Description of indicators

Area of agricultural land

This indicator covers four types of land use: total agricultural land, arable crops, permanent crops and pasture. In principle, total agricultural land is the sum of the area of arable crops, permanent crops and pasture but due to differences in the accuracy of the measurement of different land uses within countries, the sum of the components of agricultural land is not equal to the reported total agricultural land in some countries. This makes it difficult to assess changes in the components of agricultural land

Pesticide sales per hectare of agriculture land (kg of active ingredients/ha)

This indicator is expressed as the ratio of total pesticide sales in a given country to agricultural land. It is important to bear in mind that this indicator is a proxy of environmental pressure at the national level, and does not consider sub-national heterogeneity. The national figure can mask important within-country heterogeneity. Care is required when comparing pesticide sales per unit of land across countries, because of differences in crop composition, climatic conditions and farming systems, which affect the composition and intensity of usage (OECD, 2013[63]).

Additionally, pesticide sales data do not convey information on the real levels of risk for ecosystems and human health, which depend on other factors including toxicity, mobility (how quickly the substances travel through air or water) and persistence (the time chemicals remain in the air, water and food) (OECD, 2013[63]). Pesticide sales might be different from pesticide use because pesticides are sometimes stored rather than used. For some countries, pesticide sales could also include sales for urban uses (e.g. road and rail verges), private gardens, golf courses and forestry land. Most OECD countries do not have readily available indicators for risk of exposure to pesticides.

Due to changes in the methodology for collecting pesticide sales in EU countries since 2009, trends in pesticide sales could not be produced and the report will only focus on average sales levels in the period 2011-15.

Populations of a selected group of breeding bird species dependent on agricultural land for nesting or breeding (index, 2000=100)

While there are several biodiversity indicators for farmland that could potentially be tracked (OECD, 2013[63]),[1] very few are consistently collected for multiple countries. One indicator that is available for multiple countries is the farmland bird index,[2] which tracks the population of a selected group of breeding bird species that are dependent on agricultural land for nesting or breeding. Indicators based on bird populations tend to be good indicators since, given their position in the food chain, they reflect the general health and changed of ecosystems (OECD, 2013[63]). In general, a decrease in the index means that the population abundance of bird species is declining, representing biodiversity loss. If it is constant, there is no overall change. An increase implies an increase in the farmland bird population. Note that a trend in the composite index of farmland birds can hide significant changes for individual species. An increase in the index could reflect an increase in abundance of some bird species at the expense of others. The index can also be volatile over time, which could affect the assessment of its trends.

The farmland bird indicator used here mainly draws on Birdlife International's (BI) Pan European Common Bird Monitoring Scheme of the European Bird Census Council (European Birds Census Council, n.d.[64]), as well as national bird monitoring programmes. These national indices vary significantly in the number and type of species they include (ranging from 8 to 39 bird species, to reflect varying national situations), and the variety of methods used to derive the indices (see the detailed notes on OECD (2018[24]).[3]

Expanding biodiversity indicators to cover land use and habitat are needed to further strengthen the analysis and understanding of biodiversity in farmland and its interaction with other land uses. In terms of developing biodiversity indicators in farmland, some of the main conclusions of the OECD Workshop on the Use of New Technologies for Agri-environmental Indicators to Support Effective Policy Monitoring, Evaluation and Design were: data from new technologies cannot fully replace data from the field, but it can help to augment the cost-effectiveness of biodiversity monitoring on farmland and data from satellite imagery can be used to create proxy biodiversity indicators based on land cover (OECD, 2018[65]). The advantage of such an indicator is that it can be readily available and easy to standardise; an example is the Wildlife Habitat Availability indicator calculated in Canada using Earth Observations or the High Nature Value farmland for the European Union, which uses CORINE data from the Copernicus programme.

Notes

[1] Examples include biodiversity of pollinators, habitat quality indicators for biodiversity, and the genetic resources of plants and livestock.

[2] In general, indices are first calculated for each species independently at the national level using sampling results from the field, then national-level species indices are aggregated to generate a single index.

[3] As of 2018, the OECD collects farmland birds indicators directly from member countries via a questionnaire. In 2019, the data collection will include greater detail on the species and methods used to create the indicators so as to ensure comparability across countries in terms of the definition of species and the methodologies used.

2. Ammonia and greenhouse gas emissions

This chapter summarises the most recent trends in ammonia and greenhouse gas emissions (GHG) indicators, the main air pollutants from agricultural activities, from the OECD agri-environmental indicators database. It also conducts an econometric exercise to estimate the relationship between GHG emission intensities and labour productivity, and discusses how New Zealand is tackling GHG emissions intensities.

The statistical data for Israel are supplied by and under the responsibility of the relevant Israeli authorities. The use of such data by the OECD is without prejudice to the status of the Golan Heights, East Jerusalem and Israeli settlements in the West Bank under the terms of international law.

Key messages

- Trends in agricultural ammonia and greenhouse gas emissions (GHG) indicate a deterioration of agriculture's performance in the OECD area. While GHG emissions were practically unchanged in the period 1993-2005, they increased by 0.2% yearly in OECD countries from 2003 to 2015. Ammonia emissions decreased in the period 2003-15, but at a slower rate than during the period 1993-2005.

- OECD countries need to address this increase in emissions, which stems primarily from the use of synthetic fertilisers.

- The capacity of countries to produce agricultural goods while minimising GHG emissions has weakened. Although GHG emissions per dollar of agricultural production (emission intensities) continued to decline in OECD countries in the period 2003-15, it was at a slower rate than during the period 1993-2005.

- In highly productive OECD countries, continued improvements in labour productivity will not necessarily translate into a decrease in GHG emissions intensities. Indeed, these countries may be reaching a productivity level at which further improvements may induce more GHG emissions per unit of output.

- The New Zealand case study shows that reducing emission intensities, while maintaining agricultural production is possible when there are policies in place focused on research and development, particularly targeting farm profitability, productivity and emission intensity reductions in tandem with low levels of distortionary support to agriculture.

2.1. The role of agriculture on greenhouse gas and ammonia emissions

Agricultural activities affect air quality mainly via greenhouse gas (GHG) and ammonia (NH_3) emissions. It is the main emitter of methane (CH_4) and nitrous oxide (N_2O), two non-CO_2 greenhouse gases with more potential to warm the atmosphere than carbon dioxide (CO_2), but with a shorter lifespan (IPCC, 2014[1]) GHG emissions from agriculture represent 10-12% of total global GHG emissions (Smith et al., 2014[2]). Worldwide, nearly 40% of agricultural GHG emissions come from ruminants' digestive process (enteric fermentation) and 30% from agricultural soils; the remaining 30% comes from rice cultivation, biomass burning, and manure management (Tubiello et al., 2013[3]).

Agriculture's link to greenhouse gas (GHG) emissions and climate change is complex. While the sector is a contributor of GHGs to the atmosphere, agricultural soils can act as carbon sinks depending on how these are managed (OECD, 2008[4]). Agriculture is not only responsible for GHG emissions due to the direct management and operation of farms but also indirectly due to the conversion of natural habitats such as forested lands and peatlands to agricultural fields. The agricultural sector is projected to be the second sector to contribute the most to economic damages from climate change, only after losses associated with health (OECD, 2015[5]). The impacts on the sector are likely to be differentiated by space, time and crop, with some regions, especially in higher latitudes, benefitting from climate change, while regions near the Tropics will suffer the most (Smith et al., 2014[2]; OECD, 2015[5]). In some regions, higher CO_2 concentrations in the atmosphere, which tend to improve photosynthesis and increase yields, could more than compensate the potentially negative effects of hotter temperatures (Barros et al., 2015[6]; Murgida et al., 2014[7]).

Agriculture also accounts for 80-90% of total ammonia emissions globally (Bouwman et al., 1997[8]; Zhang et al., 2010[9]; Xu et al., 2019[10]) via volatilisation from livestock manure and synthetic mineral N fertiliser application (Bouwman et al., 1997[8])). Ammonia emissions are associated with two major types of environmental problems: acidification and eutrophication (OECD, 2008[4]). When combined with water in the atmosphere or after deposition, ammonia contributes to acidification of soil and water. Excess soil acidity can harm certain types of terrestrial and aquatic ecosystems. Deposition of ammonia can also increase nitrogen levels in soil and water, which may lead to eutrophication – algal and plant growth due to excess nutrients – in aquatic ecosystems (OECD, 2008[4]). Human exposure to high concentrations of NH_3 can affect the respiratory track and lung function (OECD, 2018[11]). NH_3 is also a precursor of particulate matter (PM), a potent air pollutant that poses risks to human health (OECD, 2018[12]).

Both GHG and ammonia emissions are transboundary pollutants, affecting areas beyond those where they are emitted. Therefore, international accords are paramount to effectively reducing such emissions.

2.2. Trends in GHG and ammonia emissions indicators

Agricultural GHG emissions in the OECD area are rising

Agricultural GHG emissions in the OECD area increased by 26 million tonnes of CO2 equivalent, from 1.32 Gt of CO_2 equivalent in the period 2003-05 to 1.35 Gt of CO_2 equivalent in 2013-15 (Figure 2.1). The average annual growth rate for this period was 0.2%, while the annual growth rate in the period 1993-2005 was slightly negative (-0.02%). Compared to the period 1993-2005, in the most recent period of analysis fewer countries registered negative growth rates and only five countries – Greece, Israel, Italy, Spain and the United Kingdom – had growth rates lower than -0.5%, while 21 countries did in the period 1993-2005.

The share of agriculture in total OECD GHG emissions was 9% in 2013-15. The relative contribution of agriculture in the total of national GHG emissions varies across countries, with six having a share of 15% or higher in 2013-15 (Denmark, France, Ireland, Latvia, Lithuania and New Zealand), although the contribution of these countries to the total OECD agricultural GHG emissions was low except for France (5.7%). The EU15 and the United States accounted for 66% of OECD agricultural GHG emissions in 2013-15.

Higher agricultural soil emissions explain most of the increase in GHG emissions in OECD countries during the period 2003-15 (Figure 2.2). With the exception of Iceland, Korea, Luxembourg, Mexico, Switzerland and Turkey, agricultural soil emissions accounted for more than 50% of the increase in GHG emissions in countries where these emissions increased in the period 2003-15. In the OECD area, the main GHG source that declined during this period was enteric fermentation, while manure management and agricultural soils increased. For half of the countries that saw a decrease in their GHG emissions, enteric fermentation accounted for more than 50% of that decline.

Emission intensities in OECD countries continued to decline in the period 2003-15, but at a lower speed than in the period 1993-2005. Emission intensities were 2 kg of CO_2e/USD in 1993-95, 1.8 kg of CO_2e/USD in 2003-05, and 1.7 kg of CO_2e/USD in 2013 15 (Figure 2.3). The top five countries that saw the largest decreases in emission intensities from 2003 to 2015 were Australia, Israel, Chile, New Zealand, and Spain. While in the period 1993-2005 only three countries – Latvia, Japan and the United Kingdom – increased their intensities, twelve countries did from 2003 to 2015. Moreover, four of the top five largest GHG emitters in the OECD area – France, Germany, Mexico and the United States – slowed the rate of decline in intensities in the period 2003-15; Turkey, the remaining country in the top five, increased its emissions intensity at a rate of 0.4% per year.

Figure 2.1. Agricultural GHG emissions in OECD countries are increasing

	Average agricultural GHG emissions			Change in agricultural GHG emissions		Share of agricultural GHG emissions	
	Thousand tonnes of CO$_2$ equivalent			Thousand tonnes of CO$_2$ equivalent		in national total GHG emissions (%)	in total OECD agricultural GHG emissions (%)
	1993-95	2003-05	2013-15	1993-95 to 2003-05	2003-05 to 2013-15	2013-15	2013-15
Spain	32 932	38 339	33 523	5 407	-4 816	10	2.5
Greece	9 322	9 080	8 080	-241	-1 000	8	0.6
Italy	35 196	32 595	29 475	-2 601	-3 120	7	2.2
Israel[1]	2 072	2 264	2 079	192	-184	3	0.2
United Kingdom	48 653	44 690	41 905	-3 963	-2 784	8	3.1
Denmark	12 224	11 006	10 457	-1 218	-549	20	0.8
Slovenia	1 827	1 787	1 712	-39	-75	10	0.1
Belgium	12 261	10 498	10 068	-1 763	-430	9	0.7
Australia	74 227	74 597	71 770	370	-2 827	13	5.3
EU15	373 000	354 592	341 936	-18 408	-12 656	10	25.3
Sweden	7 755	7 138	6 909	-617	-229	13	0.5
Chile[2]	13 239	13 538	13 254	300	-284	12	1.0
Slovak Republic	3 643	2 672	2 607	-972	-64	6	0.2
Norway	4 696	4 549	4 441	-146	-108	8	0.3
Ireland	19 882	19 024	18 585	-858	-439	32	1.4
France	80 398	78 985	77 560	-1 413	-1 425	16	5.7
Japan	36 812	34 757	34 190	-2 055	-567	3	2.5
New Zealand	35 579	39 850	39 312	4 271	-538	49	2.9
Canada	52 190	59 486	58 684	7 296	-802	8	4.3
Portugal	7 024	6 756	6 677	-268	-78	10	0.5
Netherlands	24 387	18 531	18 338	-5 856	-193	10	1.4
Austria	7 865	7 154	7 143	-711	-11	9	0.5
Czech Republic	9 862	7 920	7 961	-1 942	41	6	0.6
Finland	6 815	6 460	6 499	-355	39	11	0.5
Switzerland	6 397	5 936	6 005	-461	69	12	0.4
Korea	22 826	20 695	20 944	-2 131	250	3	1.5
OECD	1 330 088	1 327 300	1 354 162	-2 788	26 862	9	100
Poland	34 909	29 410	30 147	-5 499	737	8	2.2
Germany	67 541	63 648	65 994	-3 893	2 346	7	4.9
United States	505 400	526 687	549 940	21 287	23 253	8	40.6
Hungary	6 121	6 193	6 483	72	290	11	0.5
Luxembourg	745	687	721	-58	35	7	0.1
Mexico	95 307	94 412	99 971	-895	5 559	15	7.4
Lithuania	4 897	4 153	4 518	-745	365	23	0.3
Iceland	589	548	597	-41	49	13	0.0
Latvia	2 791	2 320	2 609	-472	290	23	0.2
Estonia	1 481	1 101	1 326	-380	226	7	0.1
Turkey	42 226	39 836	53 673	-2 390	13 837	12	4.0

Average annual percentage change: ▨ 2003-05 to 2013-15   ◆ 1993-95 to 2003-05

Notes: Countries are ranked in ascending order according to average annual percentage change 2003-05 to 2013-05.
1. For Israel, 1993-95 is replaced by 1996.   2. For Chile, 2013-15 is replaced by 2011-13.   Source: (OECD, 2018[13]).

Figure 2.2. Agricultural soil emissions drive GHG emissions increase in OECD countries

Percentage change in GHG emissions from 2003-05 to 2013-15

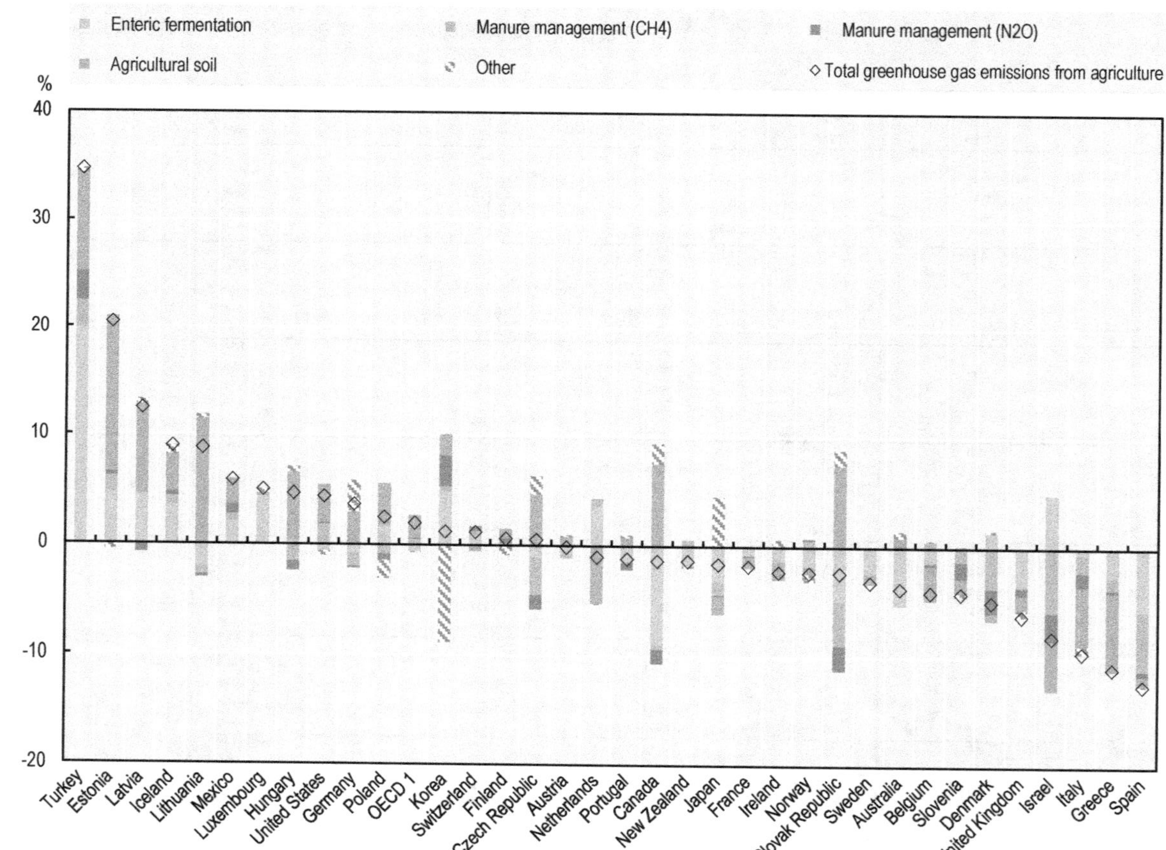

Notes: The category "other" include liming, urea application, Other carbon-containing fertilisers, Other CO_2, Rice cultivation, Prescribed burning of savannas (CH_4), Field burning of agricultural residues (CH_4), Other CH_4, Prescribed burning of savannas (N_2O), Field burning of agricultural residues (N_2O) and Other N_2O emissions sources.
1. The OECD total does not include Chile
Source: (OECD, 2018[13]).

Figure 2.3. GHG emissions intensities declined in OECD countries

	Average (kilogram of CO_2 eq. per USD)			Change in agricultural GHG emissions intensity	
	1993-95	2003-05	2013-15	1993-95 to 2003-05	2003-05 to 2013-15
Australia	3.35	2.91	2.33	-1.39	-2.20
Israel[1]	0.69	0.62	0.51	-1.16	-1.94
Chile[2]	3.18	2.49	2.16	-2.42	-1.80
New Zealand	5.41	4.80	4.03	-1.17	-1.75
Spain	1.09	0.95	0.80	-1.43	-1.70
Latvia	3.23	3.32	2.80	0.29	-1.69
United Kingdom	2.01	2.07	1.78	0.31	-1.49
Estonia	2.23	2.06	1.80	-0.81	-1.36
Mexico	3.82	2.88	2.51	-2.78	-1.35
Canada	2.49	2.36	2.07	-0.54	-1.29
Netherlands	1.49	1.26	1.11	-1.71	-1.29
Lithuania	3.12	2.64	2.37	-1.67	-1.08
Iceland	2.59	2.06	1.87	-2.28	-0.98
Norway	1.73	1.66	1.54	-0.41	-0.74
United States	2.72	2.46	2.28	-1.00	-0.74
Denmark	1.71	1.44	1.34	-1.67	-0.73
OECD[3]	2.01	1.80	1.69	-1.09	-0.65
Poland	2.18	1.84	1.73	-1.71	-0.60
Ireland	3.46	3.30	3.15	-0.48	-0.47
Germany	1.78	1.59	1.52	-1.16	-0.46
Belgium	n.a.	1.21	1.16		-0.40
Portugal	1.16	1.06	1.02	-0.88	-0.37
Switzerland	1.00	0.97	0.94	-0.31	-0.35
EU15[3]	1.67	1.58	1.53	-0.56	-0.32
Sweden	2.17	2.02	1.99	-0.72	-0.17
France	1.44	1.38	1.37	-0.41	-0.14
Austria	1.49	1.30	1.30	-1.37	0.04
Korea	0.68	0.59	0.59	-1.52	0.10
Finland	2.53	2.32	2.34	-0.87	0.11
Italy	0.76	0.68	0.69	-1.18	0.18
Greece	0.58	0.56	0.57	-0.49	0.24
Turkey	0.96	0.78	0.82	-2.04	0.45
Japan	0.39	0.41	0.43	0.64	0.45
Czech Republic	1.88	1.79	1.90	-0.50	0.62
Luxembourg	n.a.	2.52	2.76		0.93
Slovenia	2.24	2.03	2.27	-0.96	1.10
Hungary	1.08	1.06	1.18	-0.22	1.12
Slovak Republic	1.63	1.43	1.68	-1.29	1.62

Notes: Countries are ranked in descending order according to average annual percentage change 2003-05 to 2013-05. Greenhouse gas emissions are per gross production value (in constant 2004-06 USD).   1. For Israel, 1993-95 is replaced by 1996.   2. For Chile, 2013-15 is replaced by 2011-13.   3. The OECD and EU15 do not include Belgium and Luxembourg for the period 1993-95.
Sources: Greenhouse gas emissions were obtained from OECD (2018[13]) and Gross Production Value from FAOSTAT (2018[14]).

Ammonia emissions declined in OECD countries

Ammonia emissions in the OECD area decreased in the period 2003-15, but at a slower rate than during the 1993-2005 period. While a majority of countries decreased their emissions in the most recent period of analysis, Austria, Estonia, Germany, Iceland, Latvia, Luxembourg, and Switzerland reversed those trends and increased their emissions in the period 2003-15 (Figure 2.4).

International agreements to reduce emissions have played a critical role for reducing ammonia emissions. The 1999 Gothenburg Protocol to Abate Acidification, Eutrophication and Ground-level Ozone (Gothenburg Protocol) sets national ceilings for 2010/2020 for four major pollutants: sulphur emissions, nitrogen oxides (NOx), volatile organic compounds (VOCs) and ammonia (NH_3) (UNECE, 2018[15]). The ceilings were negotiated and agreed to on the basis of scientific assessments of pollution effects and abatement options. The ceilings are more stringent for Parties whose emissions have a severe environmental or health impact and for those whose emissions are relatively cheap to reduce (UNECE, 2018[15]).

To meet the targets at the national level, guidance documents and the Protocol provide a wide range of abatement techniques and measures, as well as economic instruments to reduce emissions in relevant sectors. In the case of agriculture, the Protocol establishes that within a year of the entry into force of the Protocol, signatory Parties need to take the following measures (United Nations, 2013[16]):

- establish, publish and disseminate an advisory code of good agricultural practice to control ammonia emissions
- take steps to limit ammonia emissions from the use of solid fertilisers based on urea and prohibit the use of ammonium carbonate fertilisers
- ensure that low-emissions slurry application techniques are used and that solid manure applied to land shall be ploughed and incorporated into the soil within 24 hours of spreading
- for new slurry stores on large pig and poultry farms, low-emissions storage systems will be used and for existing slurry stores on large pig and poultry farms, emissions will be reduced by 40%
- new housing systems shown to reduce emissions by 20% will be used for new animal housing on large pig and poultry farms.

Specific abatement guidelines to implement these measures were circulated by the Executive Body to the Convention on Long-range Transboundary Air Pollution. The first set of guidelines was published in 1999 and has since been updated twice as new evidence and technologies become available. The most recent guidelines include abatement recommendations pertaining to the following (UNECE, 2014[17]):

- nitrogen management, taking into account the whole N cycle
- livestock feeding strategies
- animal housing techniques
- manure storage techniques
- manure application techniques
- fertiliser application techniques
- other measures related to agricultural N
- measures related to non-agricultural and stationary sources.

Abatement strategies are presented with their potential abatement potential and their associated costs. Optimised land application of slurry and improved livestock feeding strategies tend to be the most cost-effective practices (United Nations Economic Commission for Europe, 2015[18]). Communicating practical information to farmers through guidelines has been an important factor in the adoption of such practices (Defra, 2018[19]; UNECE, 2014[17]).

Figure 2.4. Ammonia emissions declined in OECD countries

	Ammonia emissions from agriculture (thousand tonnes)			Total ammonia emissions (thousand tonnes)	Share of agriculture in total ammonia emissions (%)	Ammonia emissions from agriculture (average annual % change)	
	1993-95	2003-05	2013-15	Average 2013-15		1993-95 to 2003-05	2003-05 to 2013-15
Netherlands	243	137	107	124	86	-5.6	-2.4
Denmark	110	86	70	74	94	-2.4	-2.0
Slovak Republic	47	35	30	31	96	-2.9	-1.6
Czech Republic	106	75	65	72	90	-3.4	-1.3
Italy	437	394	346	371	93	-1.0	-1.3
Hungary	84	84	75	84	89	0.1	-1.2
Greece	65	61	55	60	91	-0.6	-1.1
Belgium	120	72	65	69	94	-4.9	-1.1
Lithuania	42	35	31	35	90	-1.9	-1.1
Spain	411	469	425	466	91	1.3	-1.0
Portugal	57	49	44	55	80	-1.6	-1.0
Poland	343	286	262	270	97	-1.8	-0.9
United States[1]	3 560	3 068	2 833	3 147	90	-1.5	-0.8
Slovenia	18	17	16	18	90	-0.4	-0.7
Finland	29	31	29	32	90	0.7	-0.6
EU15	3 198	2 942	2 816	3 047	92	-0.8	-0.4
Sweden	54	50	48	54	88	-0.8	-0.4
United Kingdom	276	245	236	273	86	-1.2	-0.4
OECD[2]	8 508	7 777	7 525	8 272	91	-0.9	-0.3
Ireland	112	111	108	109	99	-0.1	-0.3
Norway	25	27	26	28	93	0.5	-0.1
Canada	397	468	462	494	94	1.7	-0.1
France	610	590	586	521	94	-0.3	-0.1
Switzerland	61	53	53	58	93	-1.5	0.1
Austria	64	60	63	67	94	-0.6	0.4
Luxembourg	6	6	6	6	95	-1.0	0.4
Iceland	5	5	5	5	98	-0.4	0.5
Germany	604	583	630	664	95	-0.3	0.8
Estonia	12	9	11	12	89	-2.1	1.4
Latvia	15	12	14	16	84	-2.4	1.6
Turkey	453	484	593	658	90	0.7	2.0
Israel	n.a.	13	17	n.a.	n.a.		2.7
Korea[3]	143	178	233	296	79	2.2	3.0

Notes: Countries are ranked in ascending order according to average annual percentage change 2003-05 to 2013-05.
1. For the United States, data for agricultural ammonia emissions have been estimated based on the ratio agricultural ammonia/total ammonia emissions, using the share 90% as recommended by USEPA.
2. The OECD total does not include Australia, Chile, Japan, Mexico and New Zealand for both periods, and does not include Israel for 1993-95.
3. For Korea, for agricultural ammonia emissions, 1993-95 is replaced by 1990 and 2013-15 is replaced by 2012-14. For total ammonia emissions 2013-15 is replaced by 2012-14.
Source: (OECD, 2018[13]).

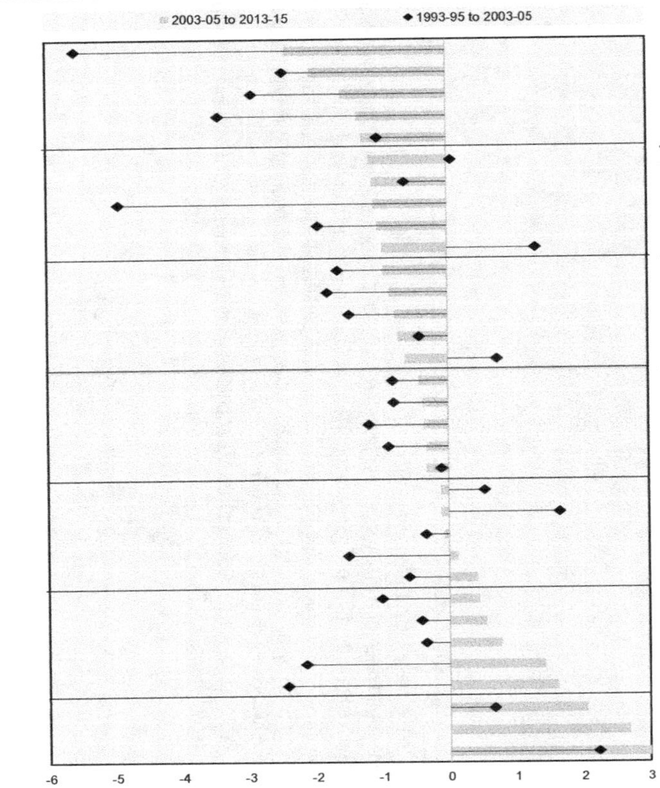

In May 2012, the UN Economic Commission for Europe agreed on the amendments to the Protocol and set up new national emission reduction commitments for main air pollutants to be achieved in 2020 and beyond (Table 2.1).

Table 2.1. Ammonia emissions reduction commitments under the Gothenburg Protocol

Party	Ammonia emissions levels 2005 (thousands of tonnes)	Reduction from 2005 level to be achieved in 2020 and beyond (%)
Austria	63	1
Belarus	136	7
Belgium	71	2
Bulgaria	60	3
Croatia	40	1
Cyprus[1,2]	5.8	10
Czech Republic	82	7
Denmark	83	24
Estonia	9.8	1
Finland	39	20
France	661	4
Germany	573	5
Greece	68	7
Hungary	80	10
Ireland	109	1
Italy	416	5
Latvia	16	1
Lithuania	39	10
Luxembourg	5	1
Malta	1.6	4
Netherlands	141	13
Norway	23	8
Poland	270	1
Portugal	50	7
Romania	199	13
Slovakia	29	15
Slovenia	18	1
Spain	365	3
Sweden	55	15
Switzerland	64	8
United Kingdom	307	8
European Union	3813	6

Notes: For Spain, figures apply to the continental European territory.

1. The information in this document with reference to "Cyprus" relates to the southern part of the Island. There is no single authority representing both Turkish and Greek Cypriot people on the Island. Turkey recognises the Turkish Republic of Northern Cyprus (TRNC). Until a lasting and equitable solution is found within the context of the United Nations, Turkey shall preserve its position concerning the "Cyprus issue".

2. The Republic of Cyprus is recognised by all members of the United Nations with the exception of Turkey. The information in this document relates to the area under the effective control of the Government of the Republic of Cyprus.

Source: Annex II of the 1999 Protocol to Abate Acidification, Eutrophication and Ground-level Ozone to the Convention on Long-range Transboundary Air Pollution (United Nations, 2013[16]).

2.3. Productive countries are reaching a levelling-off point in reducing emission intensities

To reach the goal of keeping the increase in global temperature below 2°C this century while maintaining economic growth, countries will need to reduce the emissions per unit of output (emissions intensities) in all sectors of the economy. The agricultural sector is no exception, where lowering emissions must be accompanied by output expansion to meet increasing food demand from a growing and wealthier population. A failure to do this could lead to price hikes and political unrest in certain regions of the world. In the past, productivity growth and agricultural area expansion drove food supply growth (Foley et al., 2011[20]). Demonstrating the relationship between productivity growth and emissions intensity can help to understand the role of productivity growth in tackling global warming.

In OECD countries, the growth of agricultural labour productivity is concomitant with emission intensity reductions but only up to a point; thereafter, emission intensities do not decrease and could even increase when labour productivity increases. Using the greenhouse gas emissions data from the OECD agri-environmental indicators (OECD, 2018[13]), in combination with farm labour statistics from USDA (USDA, 2018[21]) and data on agricultural gross production from FAO (FAOSTAT, 2018[14]), Figure 2.5 plots the estimated[1] association between agricultural labour productivity and a) GHG, b) CH_4 and c) N_2O and emission intensities. Emission intensity is defined as GHG emissions per dollar of value of agricultural production (Annex 2.A) and agricultural labour productivity is defined as the ratio of gross production value to the number of workers economically active in agriculture. While this indicator is only a partial productivity measure as it excludes capital and other variable inputs, it is an appropriate indicator to reflect the long-term evolution of the sector and its structural transformation as it is less responsive to changes in variable inputs (Coderoni and Esposti, 2014[22]).[2] The data used for producing the figures represent 33 countries[3] during the period 1990-2015.

The point at which the relationship between GHG, CH_4 and N_2O emission intensities and labour productivity levels off is found at a level of USD 20 000/worker (Figure 2.5). In 2015, the median labour productivity in OECD countries was USD 44 700/worker, indicating that most countries are already beyond the levelling-off point. This may suggest that further improvements in labour productivity will not necessarily translate in a decrease of emission intensities. Therefore, productivity improvements may not be enough to improve emissions intensities; specific policy action may be needed to reduce emissions per unit of output.

For GHG and CH_4, the relationship between emissions intensities and labour productivity is nonlinear and after a USD 20 000/worker level in productivity, emission intensities increase up to a given point (USD 54 000/worker), after which emissions intensities tend to decrease again. The shape of the relationship between N_2O emission intensities and labour productivity is relatively flat compared to GHG and CH_4, and, for N_2O emissions intensities, productivity improvements beyond the levelling-off point do not seem to affect emission intensities. This more moderate relationship may be driven by the fact that reductions in N_2O emission intensities are mostly driven by a decrease in the use of fertilisers, which may not necessarily translate into a labour force reduction.

Figure 2.5. GHG emissions intensities decrease with labour productivity up to a levelling-off point

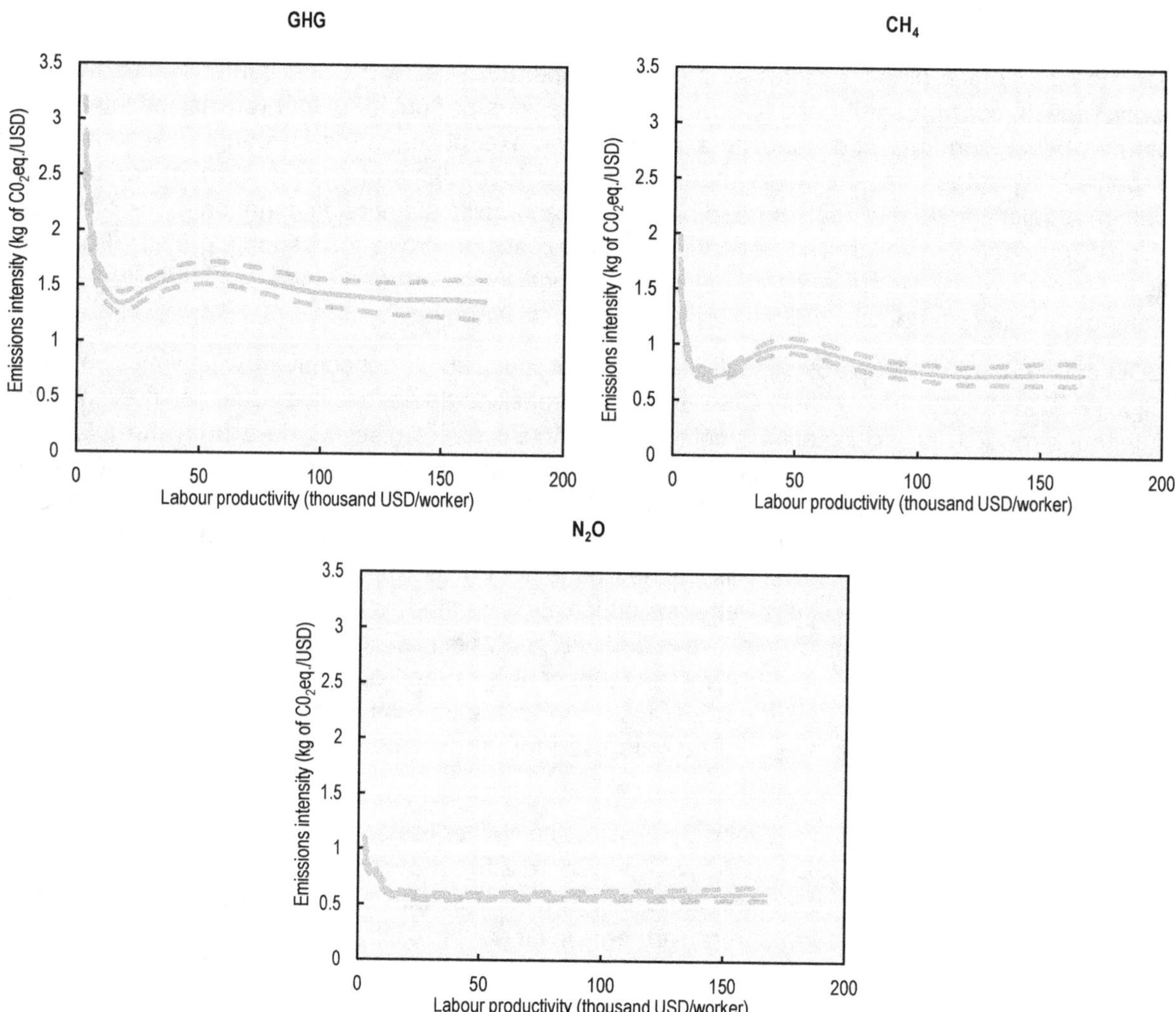

Notes: All variables were transformed to non-logged values. Dash lines show the corresponding 95% confidence intervals.
Sources: Gross Production Value was obtained from FAOSTAT (2018[14]), measured in constant 2004-2006 million USD. Agricultural labour was obtained from USDA (2018[21]), measured in 1 000 workers. Greenhouse gas emissions were obtained from the OECD Agri-environmental Indicators database (OECD, 2018[13]).

The negative nonlinear relationship between emission intensities and labour productivity is confirmed via a parametric regression analysis.[4] Increases in labour productivity are accompanied by declines in emission intensities (Table 2.2) but this negative relationship becomes less negative as productivity increases (the quadratic term is positive), reaching a turning point (the cubic term is negative) after which the relationship can become negative again. These results are consistent with Figure 2.5. There is also persistence in emission intensities: past emission intensities tend to define current intensities (*Lagged Emissions Intensity* coefficient is positive and statistically significant).

Table 2.2. Negative non-linear relationships between productivity and emissions intensities

	Dependent variable		
	GHG intensity	CH$_4$ intensity	N$_2$O intensity
Lagged emissions intensity	0.678***	0.672***	0.729***
	(0.03)	(0.029)	(0.028)
Labour productivity	-0.369***	-0.416***	-0.250***
	(0.079)	(0.086)	(0.085)
Labour productivity squared	0.110***	0.108***	0.085***
	(0.027)	(0.029)	(0.03)
Labour productivity cubic	-0.012***	-0.010***	-0.010***
	(0.003)	(0.003)	(0.003)
Trend	-0.001	-0.001	0
	(0.001)	(0.001)	(0.001)
Observations	758	760	760
Sargan test of over-identification	618.6122	653.423	622.941
	(0.73)	(0.379)	(0.846)

Notes: Coefficients were estimated using Arellano-Bond one-step GMM estimation and standard errors are shown in parentheses. *, ** and *** represent statistically significant coefficients at the 10%, 5% and 1% levels, respectively. Due to data availability, Slovenia is excluded. Belgium and Luxembourg, and the Czech Republic and the Slovak Republic are combined, respectively. Difference in observations between GHG and others comes from a lack of data on GHG emission in 2014 and 2015 for Chile. All variables were transformed into logarithms. Year dummies were included.

Sources: Greenhouse gas emissions were obtained from the OECD Agri-environmental Indicators database (OECD, 2018[13]), labour data come from USDA (2018[21]) and value of production from FAOSTAT (2018[14]).

2.4. Drivers of emission intensities declines in New Zealand

New Zealand registered one of the largest declines in greenhouse gas emissions per value of production in the OECD area, agricultural production growth, and a sharp reduction in agricultural land. This set of events are more notable considering the large share of agriculture in New Zealand's economy (7%) and its specialisation in livestock production (especially dairy products and sheep meat) (OECD, 2018[23]), a sector characterised by high emission intensities. From 1990 to 2015, the intensity of New Zealand's agricultural GHG emissions decreased 34%, a negative rate higher than both OECD average (-22%) and the average of the top 10 countries with the largest values of agricultural labour productivity (excluding New Zealand) in 1990 (-19%) (Figure 2.6). Emission intensity reductions were achieved in both N$_2$O and CH$_4$, and, in both cases, were larger than OECD countries as a whole and most productive countries as of 1990. As measured on a per unit of product (kg of meat or milk), emissions intensities have declined 20% in New Zealand's pastoral agriculture (Parliamentary Commissioner for the Environment, 2016[24]). While total GHG emissions from agriculture increased by 13% from 1990 to 2015, these would have been higher without emission intensities improvements (Ministry for the Environment, 2018[25]).

These achievements are mainly explained by three factors: 1) the adoption of policies focused on research and development, farm profitability, productivity and emissions intensity reductions; 2) changes in the production mix of animal species; and (3) low levels of distortionary support to agriculture (Henderson and Lankoski, 2019[26]). From 1990 to 2016, New Zealand became more specialised in the production of dairy products. The population of sheep decreased by 52.3% and non-dairy livestock by 23.1%, while the size of the dairy herd increased by 92.4% (Ministry for the Environment, 2018[25]). Land use for sheep, beef and deer grazing decreased by 31.6%, whereas it increased by 71.7% for dairy grazing (Ministry for the Environment, 2018[25]). New Zealand's support to farmers is one of the lowest in the OECD area (below 1% of gross farm receipts) and agricultural policies focus on key general services such as agricultural knowledge, innovation and biosecurity, which represent more than 70% of total support to agriculture (OECD, 2018[12]).

Figure 2.6. New Zealand has reduced its GHG emission intensities significantly

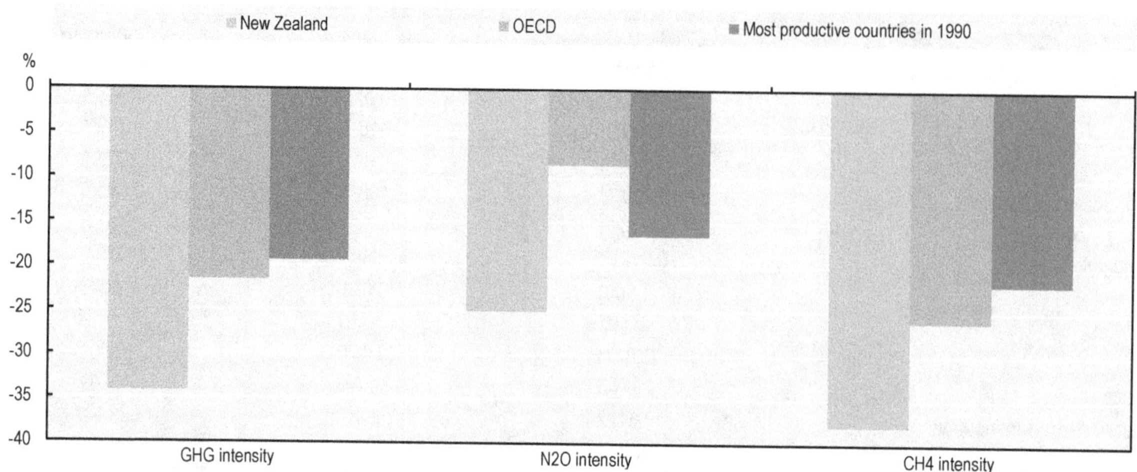

Note: Emissions intensity is the ratio of greenhouse gas emissions to agricultural gross production value.
Sources: GHG emissions were obtained from OECD AEIs (OECD, 2018[13]) and agricultural gross production value was obtained from FAOSTAT (2018[14]).

The government strongly supports innovation and technology transfers to reduce GHG emissions of the agricultural sector and is an international leader in supporting research efforts in this area. New Zealand has established dedicated institutions and R&D funding to reduce agriculture's GHG emissions, including the New Zealand Agricultural Greenhouse Gas Research Centre (www.nzagrc.org.nz), the Pastoral Greenhouse Gas Research Consortium (www.pggrc.co.nz), and the Sustainable Farming Fund. In addition, the country leads the Global Research Alliance on Agricultural Greenhouse Gases (www.globalresearchalliance.org) which aims to share knowledge and expertise on reducing GHG emissions across 56 member countries. R&D institutions in New Zealand work closely with farmers and industry to develop mitigation technologies and options that are economically attractive (Ministry for the Environment, 2017[27]); they also organise workshops, meetings and presentations with and to relevant stakeholders (Lissaman, Casey and Rowarth, 2013[28]; Kerr et al., 2013[29]; Payne, Turner and Percy, 2018[30]). Since 1990, New Zealand has reduced the emission intensities of the sector primarily by improving pasture management, nutrient management, animal selection and genetics, and animal health.

Urease inhibitors have been used as a mitigation technology since 2001 and their adoption rates have been increasing since 2014. In New Zealand, urea is the main type of nitrogen fertiliser applied to pastures; urease inhibitors restrict the action of the enzyme urease which produces ammonia emissions (Ministry for the Environment, 2018[25]). Inhibitors reduce by half the fraction of nitrogen from synthetic nitrogen fertiliser that volatilises as NH_3 (Saggar et al., 2013[31]). Urease inhibitors adoption rates have been relatively low but, since 2014, they have increased. The percentage of urea fertiliser that includes urease inhibitors sold from 2001 to 2013 in New Zealand was 6%. In 2014, the percentage increased sharply to 20% and, from 2014 to 2016, it has been 21% on average.

Looking ahead, New Zealand has clear GHG reduction targets both internationally and nationally. It set a target at -5% below 1990 levels by 2020 under the United Nations Framework Convention on Climate Change (UNFCCC), and at -11% below 1990 levels by 2030 under the Paris Agreement. In 2018, the government proposed the Zero Carbon Bill that set the national gazetted target at -50% below 1990 levels by 2050. There are currently ongoing discussions to define the future target under the Zero Carbon Bill policy.

To attain these goals, emission reductions in the agricultural sector are expected to be achieved through a combination of policies and technological improvements. The main policy instrument for reducing GHG emissions in New Zealand is the Emissions Trading Scheme (ETS). Under the ETS, agriculture has reporting obligations but not surrender obligations. The New Zealand government has projected that improvements in emissions intensities will continue and that, in combination with the implementation of the National Policy Statement for Freshwater Management (the main policy to improve water quality) and government schemes to incentivise forestry, the agricultural sector could achieve a 4.8% reduction of the projected emissions in the period 2016-30 as compared to a scenario without policy interventions (Ministry for the Environment, 2017[32]). Additional reductions (up to 10%) may be achieved by increasing adoption of readily available technologies to reduce emissions, but relevant adoption barriers such as lack of education and environmental awareness, risk aversion, and lack of trust in extension services still remain (Ministry for Primary Industries, 2018[33]).

A key question is whether the observed negative trends of emissions intensities can be maintained without affecting productivity growth. In spite of outstanding achievements in emission intensities reductions, productivity growth may be an area of concern. From 1990 to 2015, accumulated total factor productivity (TFP) growth was 40% in New Zealand; such a rate is lower relative to the one that other highly productive countries achieved over the same period (50%) (Figure 2.7). If measured by gross production value per worker, New Zealand ranked 7th (56% increase) in terms of productivity growth among the top 10 most productive countries in 1990, and that rate was almost half the average for OECD countries (109%) (Figure 2.7).

Figure 2.7. Agricultural productivity growth was modest in New Zealand relative to highly productive countries

Percentage growth, 1990-2015

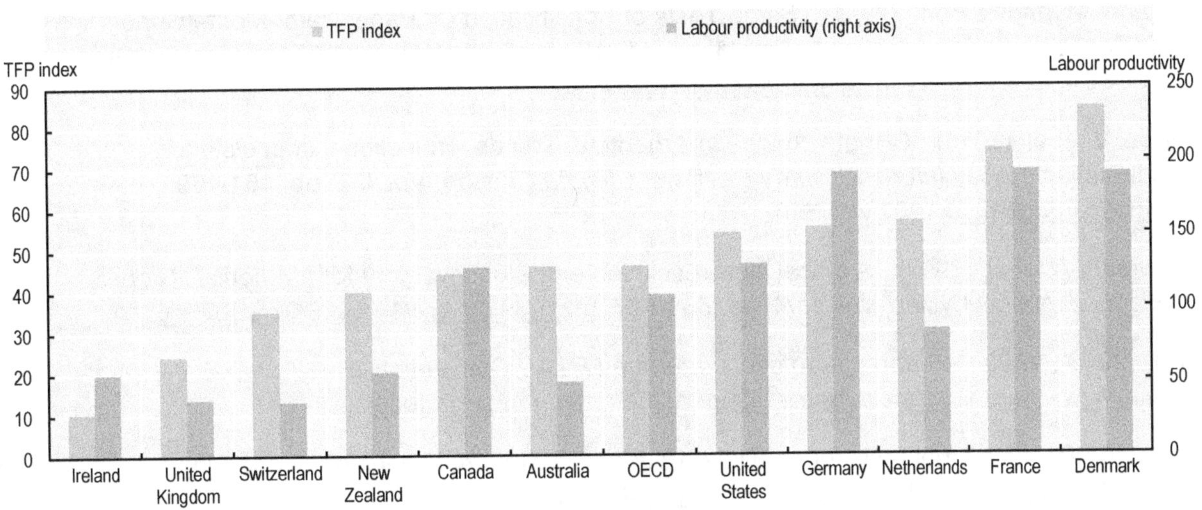

Note: Labour productivity is the ratio of agricultural gross production value to number of workers in the agricultural sector.
Sources: Agricultural gross production value was obtained from FAOSTAT (2018[14]), labour and TFP indices were obtained from USDA (2018[21]).

Notes

[1] See Annex 2.A for a detailed description of the method used for the estimation.

[2] An alternative productivity indicator is the total factor productivity index (TFP) that is produced by USDA. The TFP index measures agricultural productivity in relation to a baseline year, so its interpretation is not straightforward and comparisons between the levels of different countries are meaningless. Another drawback for its use in this setting is that it includes variable inputs such as fertiliser and feed which are subject to short-term drivers such as weather and market shocks that are not necessarily relevant to the structural transformation of agriculture (Coderoni and Esposti, 2014[22]). Moreover, the correlation between TFP and labour productivity in our dataset is relatively large (0.7), indicating that although labour productivity may be a partial measure of productivity, it is a good proxy for total factor productivity.

[3] Australia, Austria, Belgium-Luxembourg (joint due to lack of data availability), Canada, Chile, Czech Republic-Slovakia (joint due to data availability), Denmark, Estonia, Finland, France, Germany, Greece, Hungary, Iceland, Ireland, Israel, Italy, Japan, Korea, Latvia, Lithuania, Mexico, Netherlands, New Zealand, Norway, Poland, Portugal, Spain, Sweden, Switzerland, Turkey, United Kingdom, and the United States.

[4] See Annex 2.A for a detailed description of the method used for the estimation.

References

Arellano, M. and S. Bond (1991), "Some Tests of Specification for Panel Data: Monte Carlo Evidence and an Application to Employment Equations", *The Review of Economic Studies*, Vol. 58/2, p. 277, http://dx.doi.org/10.2307/2297968.   [41]

Barros, V. et al. (2015), "Climate change in Argentina: Trends, projections, impacts and adaptation", *Wiley Interdisciplinary Reviews: Climate Change*, Vol. 6/2, pp. 151-169, http://dx.doi.org/10.1002/wcc.316.   [6]

Bouwman, A. et al. (1997), "A global high-resolution emission inventory for ammonia", *Global Biogeochemical Cycles*, Vol. 11/4, pp. 561-587, http://dx.doi.org/10.1029/97GB02266.   [8]

CEIP (2019), *1999 Gothenburg protocol under the LRTAP Convention*, http://www.ceip.at/ms/ceip_home1/ceip_home/gothenburg_protocol/.   [43]

Choi, I. (2001), "Unit root tests for panel data", *Journal of International Money and Finance*, Vol. 20/2, pp. 249-272, http://dx.doi.org/10.1016/S0261-5606(00)00048-6.   [38]

Coderoni, S. and R. Esposti (2014), "Is There a Long-Term Relationship Between Agricultural GHG Emissions and Productivity Growth? A Dynamic Panel Data Approach", *Environmental and Resource Economics*, Vol. 58/2, pp. 273-302, http://dx.doi.org/10.1007/s10640-013-9703-6.   [22]

Defra (2018), *Code of Good Agricultural Practice (COGAP) for Reducing Ammonia Emissions*, http://www.nationalarchives.gov.uk/doc/open-government-licence/version/3/ (accessed on 22 January 2019).   [19]

Edenhofer, O. et al. (eds.) (2014), *Agriculture, forestry and other land use (AFOLU)*, Cambridge University Press. [2]

FAOSTAT (2018), *Value of Agricultural Production*, http://www.fao.org/faostat/en/#data/QV/metadata. [14]

Foley, J. et al. (2011), "Solutions for a cultivated planet", *Nature*, Vol. 478, pp. 337–342, http://dx.doi.org/10.1038/nature10452. [20]

Henderson, B. and J. Lankoski (2019), *Evaluating the environmental impact of agicultural policies*, http://dx.doi.org/10.1787/add0f27c-en. [26]

Im, K., M. Pesaran and Y. Shin (2003), "Testing for unit roots in heterogeneous panels", *Journal of Econometrics*, Vol. 115/1, pp. 53-74, http://dx.doi.org/10.1016/S0304-4076(03)00092-7. [42]

IPCC (2014), *Climate Change 2014: Synthesis Report. Contribution of Working Groups I, II and III to the Fifth Assessment Report of the Intergovernmental Panel on Climate Change [Core Writing Team, R.K. Pachauri and L.A. Meyer (eds.)]*. [1]

Kerr, S. et al. (2013), *Tackling Agricultural Emissions Potential Leadership from a Small Country*, http://www.motu.org.nz/publications/motu-notes (accessed on 21 January 2019). [29]

Lissaman, W., M. Casey and J. Rowarth (2013), *Innovation and technology uptake on farm*, New Zealand Grassland Association, https://www.grassland.org.nz/publications/nzgrassland_publication_2523.pdf (accessed on 24 January 2019). [28]

Ministry for Primary Industries (2018), *Report of the Biological Emissions Reference Group*, https://www.mpi.govt.nz/. [33]

Ministry for the Environment (2018), *New Zealand's Greenhouse Gas Inventory 1990–2016*, Ministry for the Environment , Wellington, New Zealand, http://www.mfe.govt.nz/sites/default/files/media/Climate%20Change/National%20GHG%20Inventory%20Report%201990-2016-final.pdf (accessed on 17 January 2019). [25]

Ministry for the Environment (2017), *New Zealand's Seventh National Communication - Fulfilling reporting requirements under the United Nations Framework convention on Climate change and the Kyoto Protocol*, http://dx.doi.org/www.mfe.govt.nz. [32]

Ministry for the Environment (2017), *The Structure of Agricultural greenhouse gas research funding in New Zealand*, https://www.nzagrc.org.nz/. [27]

Morán, M. et al. (2016), "Ammonia agriculture emissions: From EMEP to a high resolution inventory", *Atmospheric Pollution Research*, Vol. 7/5, pp. 786-798, http://dx.doi.org/10.1016/j.apr.2016.04.001. [35]

Murgida, A. et al. (2014), *Evaluación de impactos del cambio climático sobre la producción agrícola en la Argentina*, CEPAL, https://repositorio.cepal.org/bitstream/handle/11362/37197/1/LCL3770_es.pdf (accessed on 6 June 2018). [7]

Nguyen Van, P. (2005), "Distribution Dynamics of CO2 Emissions", *Environmental & Resource Economics*, Vol. 32/4, pp. 495-508, http://dx.doi.org/10.1007/s10640-005-7687-6. [36]

OECD (2018), *Agricultural Policy Monitoring and Evaluation 2018*, OECD Publishing, Paris, https://dx.doi.org/10.1787/agr_pol-2018-en. [12]

OECD (2018), *Agri-environmental indicators*, http://www.oecd.org/tad/sustainable-agriculture/agri-environmentalindicators.htm. [13]

OECD (2018), *Chapter 17. New Zealand Support to agriculture*, OECD, Paris, http://dx.doi.org/10.1787/agr-pcse-data-en. [23]

OECD (2018), *Human Acceleration of the Nitrogen Cycle: Managing Risks and Uncertainty*, OECD Publishing, Paris, https://dx.doi.org/10.1787/9789264307438-en. [11]

OECD (2015), *The Economic Consequences of Climate Change*, OECD Publishing, Paris, https://dx.doi.org/10.1787/9789264235410-en. [5]

OECD (2008), *Environmental Performance of Agriculture in OECD countries since 1990*, http://dx.doi.org/www.oecd.org/tad/env/indicators. [4]

Ordás Criado, C. (2008), "Temporal and Spatial Homogeneity in Air Pollutants Panel EKC Estimations Two Nonparametric Tests Applied to Spanish Provinces", *Environ Resource Econ*, Vol. 40, pp. 265-283, http://dx.doi.org/10.1007/s10640-007-9152-1. [37]

Parliamentary Commissioner for the Environment (2016), *Climate change and agriculture: understanding the biological greehouse gases*, http://dx.doi.org/www.pce.parliament.nz. [24]

Payne, P., J. Turner and H. Percy (2018), *A Review of the SLMACC Technology Transfer Projects*, MPI, Wellington, http://www.mpi.govt.nz/news-and-resources/publications/. [30]

Pedroni, P. (1999), "Critical Values for Cointegration Tests in Heterogeneous Panels with Multiple Regressors", *Oxford Bulletin of Economics and Statistics*, Vol. 61/s1, pp. 653-670, http://dx.doi.org/10.1111/1468-0084.0610s1653. [40]

Perman, R. and D. Stern (2003), "Evidence from panel unit root and cointegration tests that the Environmental Kuznets Curve does not exist", *Australian Journal of Agricultural and Resource Economics*, Vol. 47/3, pp. 325-347, http://dx.doi.org/10.1111/1467-8489.00216. [39]

Saggar, S. et al. (2013), "Quantification of reductions in ammonia emissions from fertiliser urea and animal urine in grazed pastures with urease inhibitors for agriculture inventory: New Zealand as a case study", *Science of the Total Environment*, Vol. 465, pp. 136-146, http://dx.doi.org/10.1016/j.scitotenv.2012.07.088. [31]

Tubiello, F. et al. (2013), "The FAOSTAT database of greenhouse gas emissions from agriculture", *Environmental Research Letters*, Vol. 8, http://dx.doi.org/10.1088/1748-9326/8/1/015009. [3]

UNECE (2018), *Protocol to Abate Acidification, Eutrophication and Ground-level Ozone*, http://www.unece.org/env/lrtap/multi_h1.html. [15]

UNECE (2014), *Guidance document on preventing and abating ammonia emissions from agricultural sources Summary*, UNECE, http://www.unece.org/fileadmin/DAM/env/documents/2012/EB/ECE_EB.AIR_120_ENG.pdf (accessed on 23 January 2019). [17]

UNFCCC (2018), *National Inventory Submissions 2018*, https://unfccc.int/process-and-meetings/transparency-and-reporting/reporting-and-review-under-the-convention/greenhouse-gas-inventories-annex-i-parties/national-inventory-submissions-2018. [34]

United Nations (2013), *1999 Protocol to Abate Acidification, Eutrophication and Ground-level Ozone to the Convention on Long-range Transboundary Air Pollution, as amended on 4 May 2012*. [16]

United Nations Economic Commission for Europe (2015), *Framework Code for Good Agricultural Practice for Reducing Ammonia Emissions*. [18]

USDA (2018), *International Agricultural productivity*, https://www.ers.usda.gov/data-products/international-agricultural-productivity. [21]

Xu, R. et al. (2019), "Global ammonia emissions from synthetic nitrogen fertilizer applications in agricultural systems: Empirical and process-based estimates and uncertainty", *Global Change Biology*, Vol. 25, pp. 314–326, https://doi.org/10.1111/gcb.14499. [10]

Zhang, Y. et al. (2010), "Agricultural ammonia emissions inventory and spatial distribution in the North China Plain", *Environmental Pollution*, Vol. 158/2, pp. 490-501, http://dx.doi.org/10.1016/j.envpol.2009.08.033. [9]

Annex 2.A. Description of indicators

Agricultural greenhouse gas emissions (thousand tonnes)

The data to create this indicator was obtained from the United Nations Framework Convention on Climate Change (UNFCCC) database on national inventory reports (NIR) (UNFCCC, 2018[34]) for OECD countries included in Annex I of the UNFCCC. For OECD countries not included in Annex 2.B, data were compiled directly by the OECD via a questionnaire. While the UNFCCC requires countries to use a standard reporting format (CRF) for tables to ensure robust and standardised reporting, estimates made by individual countries may vary depending on factors and methods used in their own calculations. In addition, assumptions made in agricultural GHG emission calculations simplify complex agricultural systems, thereby introducing uncertainty into the estimate of GHG emissions. Although the OECD questionnaire for its member countries not included in Annex I follows the CRF tables to facilitate the treatment of the responses, the same caveats apply.

The categories covered according to the IPCC nomenclature are: 3A-Enteric fermentation, 3B-Manure management, 3C-Rice cultivation, 3D-Agricultural soil, 3E-Prescribed burning of savannas, 3F- Field burning of agricultural residues, 3G-Liming, 3H-Urea application, 3I-Other carbon-containing fertilisers, 3J – Others.

Intensity of agricultural greenhouse gas emissions (kg of CO_2 equivalent/USD)

This indicator measures agricultural emissions of greenhouse gases per agricultural gross production value. It helps to assess whether agricultural production value is decoupled with greenhouse gas emissions of the sector. Agricultural gross production value measures production in monetary terms at the farm gate level and it is calculated by multiplying gross production quantities by output prices at farm gate (FAOSTAT, 2018[14]). Since intermediate uses within the agricultural sector (seed and feed) have not been subtracted from production data, this value of production aggregate refers to the notion of "gross production" (FAOSTAT, 2018[14]). It is important to recognise that distortionary policies such as market price support may affect the gross production value because it is measured at the farm gate level. A more appropriate measure of value would use non-distorted international prices; however, no such dataset is available at the global level.

Ammonia emissions (thousand tonnes)

Ammonia emissions for OECD countries were obtained from data officially submitted by the Parties to the Convention on Long Range Transboundary Air Pollution (CLRTAP) to the European Monitoring and Evaluation Programme (EMEP) programme via the United Nations Economic Commission for Europe (UNECE). Emissions reported under the CLRTAP tend to follow a bottom-up approach: they are calculated by applying emissions factors to geo-localised farm activities (Morán et al., 2016[35]). While reporting under the CLRTAP ensures standardised formats and facilitates consistency, there could be differences in terms of emissions factors and methodologies used across countries. Moreover, emissions are known to vary through the year and a national figure can mask spatial heterogeneity within countries (OECD, 2018[11]).

Annex 2.B. Econometric model

This annex provides further details on the empirical analysis of labour productivity and GHG emissions intensities. Table 2.B.1 shows descriptive statistics of the data used, which includes 33 countries in the period 1990-2015.

Annex Table 2.B.1. Descriptive statistics

Variable	Observations	Mean	Std. Dev.	Minimum	Maximum
Labour productivity (USD1 000/worker)	828	34.867	28.320	2.614	167.456
GHG emissions intensity (kg of CO2e/USD)	880	1.841	0.987	0.374	5.856
N2O emissions intensity (kg of CO2e/USD)	882	0.744	0.407	0.111	2.360
CH4 emissions intensity (kg of CO2e/USD)	882	1.051	0.698	0.195	4.645

Sources: Agricultural gross production value was obtained from FAOSTAT (2018[14]), labour data were obtained from USDA (2018[21]) and GHG emissions data from the OECD Agri-environmental Indicators Database (OECD, 2018[13]).

Figure 2.5 was estimated using non-parametric methods. Non-parametric methods are suitable for this analysis because they do not assume a particular shape of the relationship between the outcome and the covariates (Nguyen Van, 2005[36]; Ordás Criado, 2008[37]). The method consists on running a number of local regressions at different values of the covariates with an optimal bandwidth. The density of the outcome is estimated by using the Epanechnikov Kernel function. A rule-of-thumb estimator selects the optimal bandwidth. Only two variables are used, agricultural labour productivity versus emission intensities (GHG, CH_4 and N_2O), to create the graphs in Figure 2.5.

The parametric model is as follows:

$$e_{kit}^{GPV} = \alpha_i + \beta_{k1} p_{it}^L + \beta_{k2} (p_{it}^L)^2 + \beta_{k3} (p_{it}^L)^3 + t + u_{kit},$$

$$u_{kit} = \gamma_{ki} + \eta_{kit},$$

This model requires that variables are stationary or at least cointegrated so that the relationship obtained in the parametric regression is not merely spurious. First, panel unit root tests are conducted to test for stationarity (Choi, 2001[38]; Perman and Stern, 2003[39]; Coderoni and Esposti, 2014[22]). Three variables – namely labour productivity, GHG emission intensity, and CH_4 emission intensity– do not reject the null hypothesis of containing unit roots (hence are not stationary) even at 10% level; they become stationary when first differences are taken (Table 2.B.2).

Annex Table 2.B.2. Unit root test

	Estimate	P-Value		Estimate	P-Value
Labour productivity (GPV/L)	-4.577	1.000	Δ Labour productivity GPV/L	46.563	0.000
GHG emissions intensity	0.719	0.236	Δ GHG emissions intensity	52.952	0.000
N2O emissions intensity	2.907	0.002	Δ N2O emissions intensity	49.162	0.000
CH4 emissions intensity	0.497	0.310	Δ CH4 emissions intensity	55.931	0.000

Notes: Fisher type augmented Dickey-Fuller tests (F-ADF) are conducted. Null hypothesis is containing unit roots in all panels and the alternative is at least one individual in the panel is stationary. We do not include a trend and one lag is used in the ADF regressions. In addition, the Im-Pesaran-Shin test is performed (Im, Pesaran and Shin, 2003[40]) and produces similar results as F-ADF tests.

Provided those three variables have unit roots in levels, cointegration tests are then performed to check for long-term relationships (Pedroni, 1999[40]). According to the results in Table 2.B.3, all the tests, except group ρ, are significant at the 5% level for both GHG and CH_4 emission intensities. Hence, there exists a cointegrating relationship between GHG and CH_4 emission intensities with first, second and third power of labour productivity.

Annex Table 2.B.3. Cointegration tests

Test statistics	GHG emissions intensity		CH₄ emissions intensity	
	Panel	Group	Panel	Group
v	3.003		2.726	
	(0.001)		(0.003)	
ρ	-2.591	-1.041	-1.708	-0.203
	(0.005)	(0.149)	(0.044)	(0.420)
t	-7.116	-8.414	-5.878	-7.201
	(0.000)	(0.000)	(0.000)	(0.000)
ADF	-4.727	-5.189	-3.353	-4.850
	(0.000)	(0.000)	(0.000)	(0.000)

Notes: Data for 1996 and 2000 of Israel are excluded, as cointegration tests do not allow gaps. All statistics are distributed as N(0,1). Rejecting the null of no cointegration is one-sided. Panel v is non-parametric variance ratio statistic, ρ is non-parametric test statistic, t and ADF (augmented Dickey-Fuller) are parametric statistic. Time dummies included.

Given these results, the preferred model is a dynamic model as it can capture the processes of adjustment to the long-run equilibrium as indicated by the results of the cointegration test. The estimated model is the Arellano-Bond one-step GMM estimation (Arellano and Bond, 1991[41]). The dynamic model generally includes lagged dependent variables as explanatory variable as follows:

$$e_{kit}^{GPV} = \alpha_{ki} + \varphi_{ki} e_{ki,t-1}^{GPV} + \beta_{k1} p_{it}^{L} + \beta_{k2} (p_{it}^{L})^2 + \beta_{k3} (p_{it}^{L})^3 + trend + year + u_{kit},$$

where variables are indexed over the types of emission k, country i, and year t. The dependent variable e_{kit}^{GPV} is the log of emission intensity. The independent variables are the log of agricultural labour productivity p_{it}^{L} and its squared and cubed terms. α_{ki} is the intercept. $u_{kit} = v_i + \varepsilon_{kit}$ is the error term composed of a panel-level effects component (v_i) and an error term i.d.d. over the whole sample (ε_{kit}) and m is the maximum length of lag. A trend ($trend$) and year dummies ($year$) have also been included.

Arellano-Bond GMM uses instruments to deal with endogeneity between the lag of the dependent variable and the error term. We perform the one-step GMM estimation which assumes homoscedasticity on the disturbance term u_{kit}. For model specification, AR(2) test for serial correlation and Sargan test for over-identification.

Since autocorrelation of order 2 was not ruled out, for robustness check, results from a static random-effects model are displayed in Table 2.B.4. Results support the nonlinear and negative relationship between labour productivity and emissions intensities.

Annex Table 2.B.4. Static model

	Dependent variable: Emissions intensity		
	GHG	N₂O	CH₄
Labour productivity	-1.111***	-0.814*	-1.274***
	(0.279)	-0.445	(0.250)
Labour productivity Squared	0.353***	0.310**	0.357***
	(0.099)	-0.152	(0.086)
Labour productivity Cubic	-0.036***	-0.036**	-0.033***

	Dependent variable: Emissions intensity		
	(0.011)	-0.017	(0.010)
Trend	0.001***	-0.004	0.004
	(0.000)	-0.01	(0.011)
Observations	826	828	828
Number of Countries	33	33	33
R-squared	0.562	0.343	0.609

Notes: All variables were transformed into logarithms. Coefficients were estimated using a random effect model and robust standard errors are reported in parentheses. *, ** and *** represent statistically significant coefficients at the 1%, 5% and 10% levels, respectively. Year dummies are included.

Sources: Gross Production Value was obtained from FAOSTAT (2018[14]) and agricultural labour was obtained from USDA (2018[21]). GHG emissions data come from the OECD agri-environmental indicators database (OECD, 2018[13]).

3. Nutrient balances in agriculture

This chapter analyses the trends of nutrient balances in OECD countries and discusses the role of crop mix, livestock composition, improved practices, technological innovations, and policies on nutrient surpluses. An econometric estimation of the determinants of nutrient balances in OECD countries is undertaken and the policy lessons from Korean and Danish experiences fighting high levels of nutrient surpluses distilled.

The statistical data for Israel are supplied by and under the responsibility of the relevant Israeli authorities. The use of such data by the OECD is without prejudice to the status of the Golan Heights, East Jerusalem and Israeli settlements in the West Bank under the terms of international law.

Key messages

- Since 2000, OECD countries have on average experienced declining trends in nutrient surpluses. Although almost all OECD countries recorded a decrease in phosphorus surpluses, the picture is mixed in the case of nitrogen due to increased nitrogen fertiliser application rates. For some countries, progress in reducing nutrient surpluses has deteriorated, and nutrient balances have even increased in the last decade.

- Reduced phosphorus fertiliser application rates seem to be the main driver of reduced phosphorus surpluses, although livestock, crop-mix changes, and policy interventions are associated with reductions in both nitrogen and phosphorus nutrient balances. Phosphorus fertiliser application rates fell for most OECD countries, possibly as a result of improved farm practices.

- In the last decade, the rates of decline in phosphorus surpluses have accelerated while they have decelerated for nitrogen, raising concerns about the ability of OECD countries to maintain nitrogen surpluses reductions in the future.

- In several countries that have reduced their nitrogen surpluses, changes in livestock composition and crop mix played a role. In particular, an increase in oil crops as a share of total harvested crops and a decrease in cattle as a share of total livestock significantly reduced nutrient surpluses.

- Technological innovations used in precision agriculture have the potential to reduce nutrient surpluses. Enhanced efficiency nitrogen fertilisers can improve crop uptake of nitrogen and reduce the risk of nitrogen leaching. The ultimate environmental impact of these technologies, however, is highly dependent on the type of crop and the biophysical conditions of the farm, as well on other management practices.

- Distortionary support policies seem to be associated with larger surpluses, while countries that adopted policies targeting nitrogen pollution also reduced both nitrogen and phosphorus surpluses.

- Korea and Denmark show how two different approaches to reducing nutrient surpluses can be effective. Korea has gradually removed distortionary agricultural support polies, while Denmark acted early and persistently to adopt a mix of policies with aligned objectives and clear targets on reducing both nitrogen and phosphorus, combined with monitoring and evaluating the impact of policies to improve their effectiveness.

3.1. The role of nutrients in agriculture and their environmental impacts

Phosphorus (P) and nitrogen (N) are essential nutrients for supporting plant growth. Nitrogen is necessary for protein build-up and phosphorus is required for energy use and transfer (Conley et al., 2009[1]). Nutrient inputs in agriculture are thus fundamental to maintaining and increasing crop and forage productivity (OECD, 2013[2]). Agricultural areas with sustained nutrient deficits may suffer reductions in soil fertility, while nutrient surpluses are likely to contribute to water and air pollution (OECD, 2013[2]; OECD, 2008[3]).

A complex range of physical processes drives the nutrient cycle in the environment (OECD/EUROSTAT, 2012[4]; OECD/EUROSTAT, 2012[5]). Agricultural activities contribute to nutrient build-up and have significantly affected nutrient cycles (Liu et al., 2010[6]). Fertiliser use and manure application are some of the most significant ways agriculture supplies nutrients to the environment. While some of those nutrients are taken up by crops and forage, nutrient inputs exceed nutrient outputs on most agricultural lands, thereby creating nutrient surpluses (Liu et al., 2010[6]; Bouwman, 2013[7]).

Nitrogen is an abundant element in the atmosphere, mainly present in gas form. It is a key nutrient for crop growth, and is added in inorganic fertilisers and manure. It is estimated that 40% to 60% of N fertiliser is absorbed by crops and the remainder is lost in the environment (Sebilo, 2013[8]). Some nitrogen stays in the soil and some volatilises during and shortly after fertiliser applications and manure spreading in the form of ammonia (NH_3) and nitric oxide (NO) (Mosier et al., 1998[9]). Ammonia volatilisation also occurs after animal excretion and during storage of livestock manure. Nitrogen is highly mobile and can reach groundwater reservoirs by leaching; it can also reach surface water via runoff.

An excess of nitrogen in surface water leads to excessive plant and algal growth, producing eutrophication. Eutrophic water bodies can suffer biodiversity losses and fish deaths. Nitrate concentrations in groundwater pose risks to livestock and human health. Nitrogen volatilisation contributes to higher concentrations of nitrous oxide (N_2O), a potent greenhouse gas, and can lead to soil and water acidification, potentially affecting crop yields and biodiversity (Goulding, 2016[10]).

In contrast to nitrogen, phosphorus sources are naturally limited as phosphorus comes from mineral sources. Phosphorus uptake rates by plants are estimated to be relatively low, between 10% to 15%; the remainder stays in the soil or ends up in water bodies (Roberts, 2015[11]). Phosphorus is relatively immobile so it can remain in the soil for years. Soil P retention depends on several soil characteristics. In many OECD countries, phosphorus application rates have been declining because soils are already P saturated (OECD, 2013[2]).

Phosphorus deficiency in the soil can lead to declining fertility in areas under crop or forage production (OECD, 2008[3]; OECD, 2013[2]). In contrast, a phosphorus surplus is associated with environmental risks as excess P can lead to surface water contamination due to runoff and soil erosion (EUROSTAT, 2017[12]; Bomans E., 2005[13]). While phosphorus concentrations in water do not pose a direct risk to human health, they are an indirect risk as they favour the growth of cyanobacteria and algal blooms in bodies of water. An excess of algae in water bodies diminishes the amount of oxygen available for other organisms and leads to biodiversity losses and fish deaths. Cyanobacteria can produce toxic substances that can affect human and animal health (Chorus, 1999[14]; Hitzfeld, 2000[15]).

3.2. Trends in nutrient balance indicators

Overall, nutrient surpluses (see description of indicators in Annex 3.A) show a decreasing trend in OECD countries since 1992. From 1992 to 2014, the average nitrogen surplus fell from 85 kg/ha to 67kg/ha (Figure 3.1) and the phosphorus surplus from 13 kg/ha to 6 kg/ha (Figure 3.2). Although almost all countries recorded a reduction in their phosphorus surplus over the analysed period, the picture is more mixed for nitrogen balances.

While the nitrogen surplus in OECD countries overall has decreased since 1992, the pace of the reduction has slowed over the period 2002-14. Australia, Austria, Iceland, Italy, Japan, Latvia, Mexico, Norway, Portugal, Slovak Republic and Turkey even reversed the declining trends seen in the period 1992-2004 and exhibited positive growth rates in the last decade (Figure 3.1). Notably, this happened in countries that already had high levels of N surplus per hectare, such as Japan and Norway.

Since 2002, OECD countries have enhanced their efforts to reduce phosphorus surpluses. The P surplus for OECD countries fell, on average, more quickly in the period 2004-14 (4.1%) than the period 1992-2002 (3%) (Figure 3.2), signalling these increased efforts. Almost all countries exhibited a steeper downward trend in the most recent period analysed. Only a few countries, such as Austria, Iceland, Mexico and Turkey, reversed the reduction they experienced in the 1990s and increased their surpluses per hectare in the 2000s.

Figure 3.1. Nitrogen balance per hectare of agricultural land in OECD countries, 1992-2014

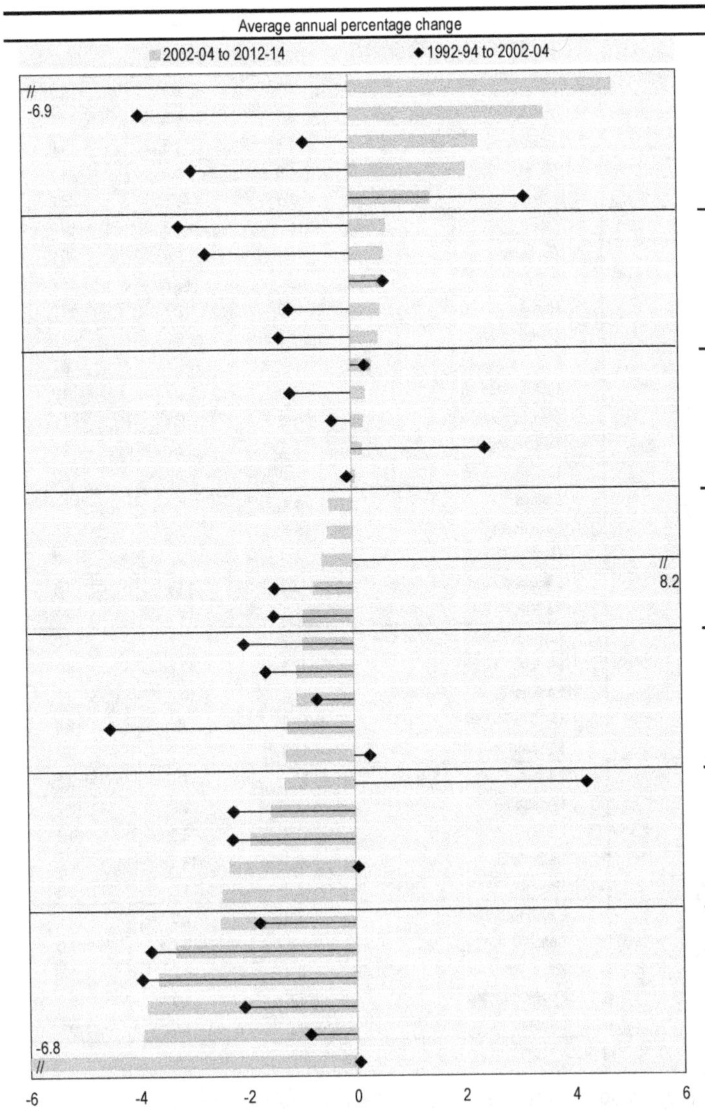

Average annual percentage change		Average (kg nitrogen/ha)		
■ 2002-04 to 2012-14 ◆ 1992-94 to 2002-04		1992-94	2002-04	2012-14
Latvia		34	17	27
Austria		40	27	38
Iceland		7	7	9
Slovak Republic		50	37	46
New Zealand		33	46	53
Turkey		33	24	25
Portugal [1]		45	37	39
Poland		42	45	48
Norway		102	91	96
Australia		20	18	19
Korea		234	240	249
Mexico		26	23	23
Japan		179	173	176
Czech Republic		58	74	76
Italy		72	72	72
Israel		n.a.	132	127
Hungary		n.a.	38	36
Canada		14	30	28
Switzerland [2,5]		74	64	60
OECD [3]		85	73	67
United Kingdom [4]		84	71	65
Luxembourg		166	141	127
Germany [5]		107	100	91
Belgium		246	156	138
United States		34	35	31
Spain		31	47	41
Finland		67	54	46
EU15		107	85	70
France		60	61	48
Estonia [6]		n.a.	30	24
Slovenia		88	73	57
Netherlands		304	207	148
Denmark		180	121	83
Sweden [5]		57	46	32
Greece		89	82	55
Ireland [5]		60	60	32

Notes: n.a. Not available. Balance (surplus or deficit) expressed as kg nitrogen per hectare of total agricultural land.

Countries are ranked in descending order according to average annual percentage change 2002-04 to 2012 14.

1. For Portugal, 1992-94 is replaced by 1995-97.

2. For Switzerland, total agricultural area includes summer grazing.

3. The OECD total does not include Chile, Estonia, Hungary and Israel.

4. For the United Kingdom, 1992-94 is replaced by 1995.

5. For Germany, Ireland, Sweden and Switzerland, 2012-14 is replaced by 2011-13.

6. For Estonia, 2002-04 is replaced by 2004-06.

Source: OECD (2018[16]).

Figure 3.2. Phosphorus balance per hectare of agricultural land in OECD countries, 1992-2014

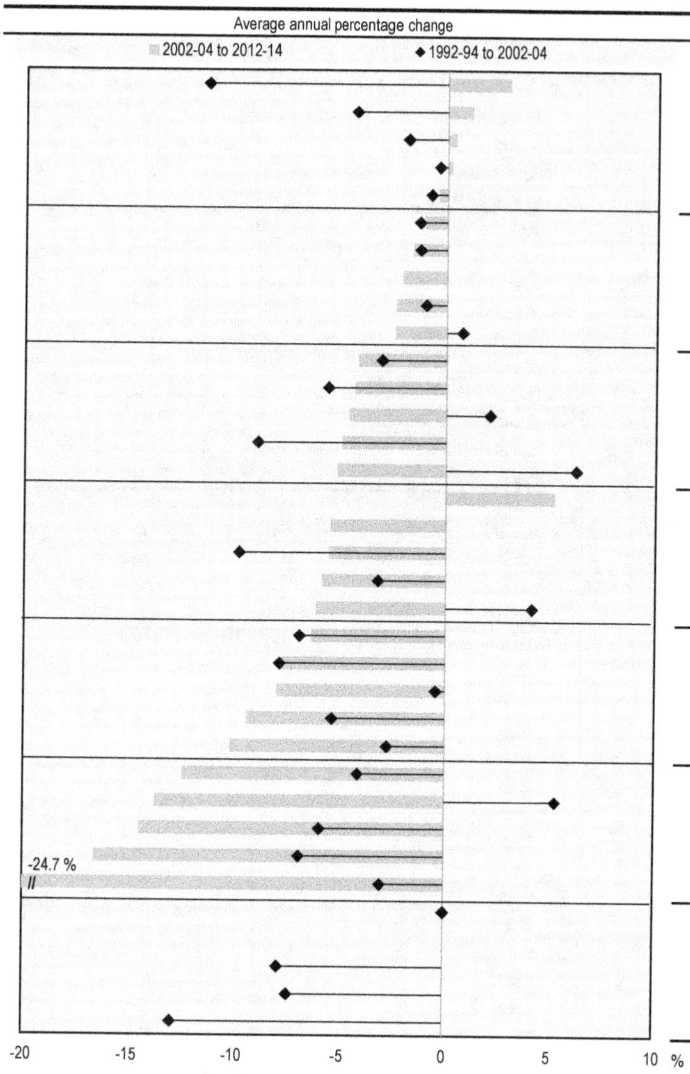

	Average (kg phosphorus/ha)		
	1992-94	2002-04	2012-14
Austria	6.7	2.0	2.7
Turkey	9.7	6.3	7.0
Iceland	1.9	1.5	1.6
Mexico	1.8	1.7	1.7
Korea	52.5	48.5	46.6
Japan	75.7	66.3	59.7
Australia	1.1	1.0	0.9
Israel	n.a.	43.7	35.6
Norway	14.0	12.7	10.0
United States	3.4	3.7	2.9
OECD [1]	12.8	9.4	6.2
United Kingdom [2]	9.0	5.7	3.7
New Zealand	9.8	12.1	7.6
Switzerland [3, 4]	9.3	3.7	2.3
Spain	4.0	7.3	4.3
Estonia [5]	n.a.	-4.7	-7.0
Luxembourg	n.a.	7.0	4.0
Germany [4]	9.3	3.3	2.0
Denmark	18.3	13.3	7.3
Poland	3.3	5.0	2.7
Finland	15.7	7.7	4.0
Belgium	28.7	12.7	5.7
Portugal [6]	11.0	10.7	4.7
EU15 [7]	12.8	7.4	2.8
Slovenia	14.0	10.7	3.7
Ireland [4]	11.7	7.7	2.3
Canada	1.8	2.9	0.7
France	11.7	6.3	1.3
Netherlands	33.3	16.3	2.7
Greece	7.7	5.7	0.3
Czech Republic	2.0	2.0	-0.7
Hungary	n.a.	0.7	-1.0
Italy	8.3	3.7	-1.7
Slovak Republic [8]	2.0	1.0	-0.7
Sweden [4]	4.0	1.0	-0.7

The left panel shows the average annual percentage change, with bars for 2002-04 to 2012-14 and diamonds for 1992-94 to 2002-04, plotted on an axis from -20 to 10 %. One value is marked -24.7 %.

Notes: n.a. Not available. Balance (surplus or deficit) expressed as kg phosphorus per hectare of total agricultural land.
Countries are ranked in descending order of their average annual percentage change 2002-04 to 2012 14.
1. The OECD total does not include Chile, Estonia, Hungary, Israel and Luxembourg.
2. For the United Kingdom, 1992-94 is replaced by 1995.
3. In the case of Switzerland, total agricultural area includes summer grazing.
4. For Germany, Ireland, Sweden and Switzerland, 2012-14 is replaced by 2011-13.
5. For Estonia, 2002-04 is replaced by 2004-06. The average annual percentage change refers to change in phosphorus deficit.
6. For Portugal, 1992-94 is replaced by 1995-97.
7. EU15 does not include Luxembourg.
8. For the Slovak Republic, 1992-94 is replaced by 1993-95.
Source: OECD (2018[16]).

Several countries that significantly reduced the growth rates of N surpluses from the period 1992-2002 to 2002-14 also reduced the growth of P surpluses. For countries such as Canada, France, Greece, Ireland, New Zealand, Slovenia, Spain, and the United States, progress in reducing the growth rates of N surpluses between the first and latest periods analysed has been accompanied by similar progress in P surplus trends.

On average, OECD countries reduced N inputs due to reduced manure inputs and despite increased N inputs from fertiliser. In parallel, crop uptake significantly increased, further lowering the overall N surplus. For most countries that experienced reductions in N surpluses in the period 2002-04 to 2012-14, fertiliser and net inputs of manure also declined. Some countries, such as Canada, Estonia, Hungary, Israel and the United States, increased both inputs and outputs, but the rate of change in N outputs was large enough to compensate for the increase in N inputs (Figure 3.3), leading to overall reductions in N surpluses in those countries.

Figure 3.3. Contribution of specific nitrogen inputs and outputs to total changes in nitrogen surplus, 2002-14

Percentage change between 2002-04 and 2012-14

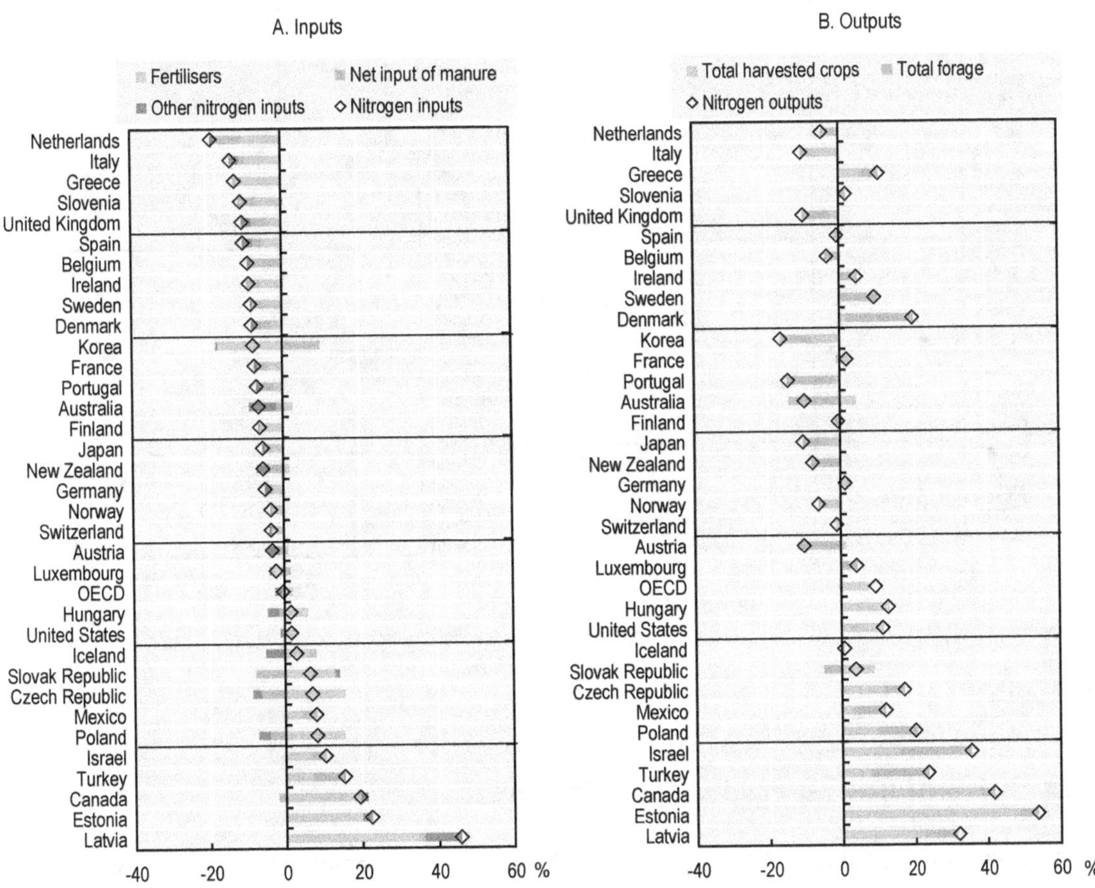

Note: For EU countries, Norway, the OECD and Switzerland, output category "nutrient removal by crop residues removed from the field" is not shown on the graph.
Source: OECD (2018[16]).

Fertiliser was the main component driving the reduction in P surpluses. Most OECD countries, with the exception of Canada, Latvia, Mexico and Turkey, saw reductions in P inputs in the period 2002-2004 to 2012-2014 (Figure 3.4). Declining fertiliser use and higher P crop uptake explain most of the reductions in P inputs and surplus. Interestingly, most countries that experienced increases in P input also experienced N input growth.

Figure 3.4. Contribution of specific phosphorus inputs and outputs to total changes in phosphorus surplus, 2002-14

Percentage change between 2002-04 and 2012-14

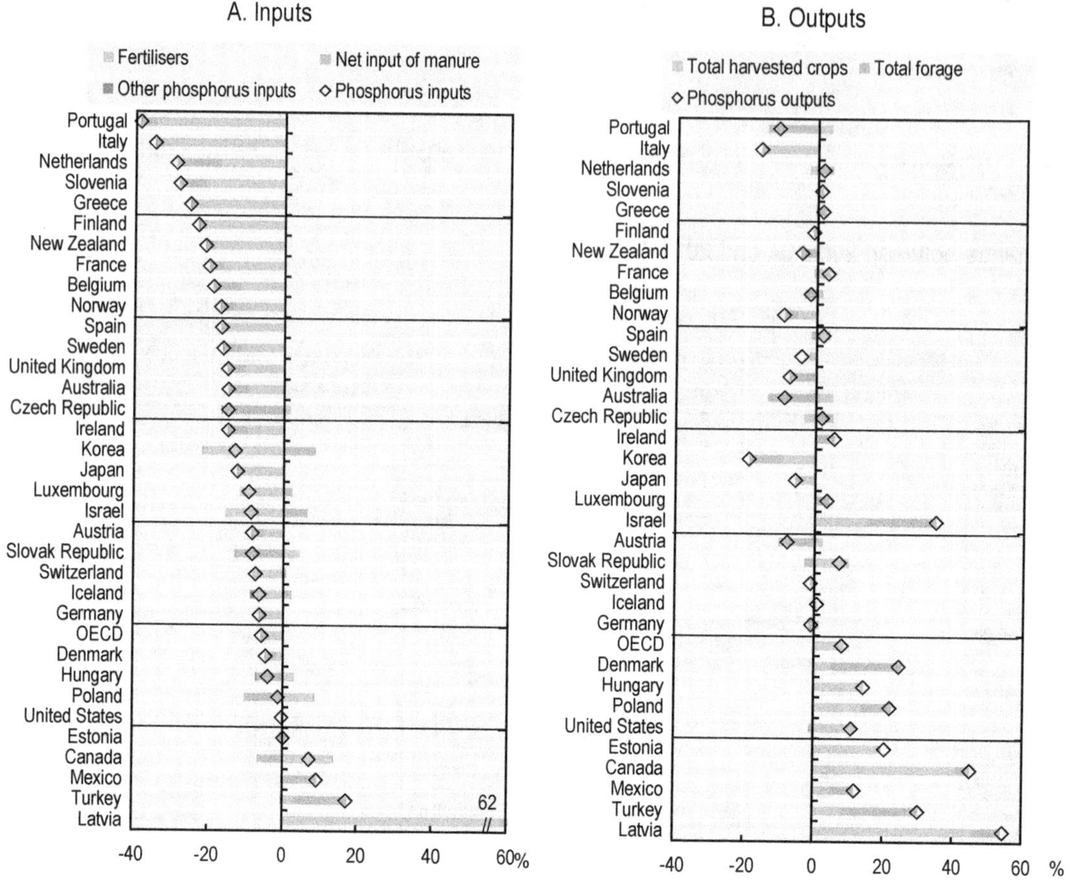

Note: For EU countries, Norway, the OECD and Switzerland, output category "nutrient removal by crop residues removed from the field" is not shown on the graph.
Source: OECD (2018[16]).

3.3. Key drivers of nutrient balance indicators

This section relates the observed trends in nutrient balances to potential drivers. The existing literature identifies three key drivers: livestock composition, crop mix and the adoption of improved cultivars, agricultural policies, and management practices. For each driver, an attempt is made to empirically relate nutrient balance indicators to variables that reflect those drivers.

Livestock composition and crop mix

Livestock density and livestock composition are relevant to nutrient surpluses. Cattle usually have higher N and P excretion rates (kg per animal) than pigs and poultry (Sebek et al., 2014[17]; Velthof, Hou and Oenema, 2015[18]), with dairy cows having the highest rates among cattle. The crop mix in a given country is another crucial factor, which is in turn influenced by demand and trade policies (Billen, Lassaletta and Garnier, 2015[19]). The N uptake of oil crops is relatively high compared to other crops such as cereals and fruits and vegetables (Zhang et al., 2015[20]).

To better relate changes in the crop mix and livestock composition to changes in inputs and outputs observed in the period 2002-14 (Figure 3.3 and Figure 3.4), t tests of equality of annual growth rates of livestock densities and cropland types over the same period were performed, comparing countries that increased their inputs or outputs, and those that decreased them. Table 3.1 and Table 3.2 display the results for nitrogen and phosphorus respectively.

Countries that increased their N inputs also increased the area under oil crops at a higher rate (6.5% per year) than those that decreased their N inputs (2.7% per year) and the difference is statistically significant at the 5% level (Table 3.1). In the case of N outputs, there were statistically significant differences between the growth rates in the areas cultivating oil crops and fruit and vegetables, as well as livestock densities, between countries that increased versus those that decreased N outputs. Countries that increased N uptake experienced a stronger expansion in the area of oil crop cultivation, a larger decrease in the area of fruit and vegetable cultivation, and a reduction in livestock density, compared to countries that reduced N uptake.

Table 3.1. Differences in livestock density and crop mix for countries that increased versus those that decreased N inputs and outputs

	Inputs			Outputs		
Change in input/output	Observations	Mean of annual growth rates	Difference (mean decrease- mean increase)	Observations	Mean of annual growth rates	Difference (mean decrease- mean increase)
	Oil crops (ha)			Oil crops (ha)		
Decrease	264	0.027	-0.04**	168	0.011	-0.05***
Increase	216	0.065		312	0.062	
	Fruit and vegetables (ha)			Fruit and vegetables (ha)		
Decrease	264	-0.002	0.02	168	-0.001	0.01***
Increase	216	-0.022		312	-0.017	
	Cereals (ha)			Cereals (ha)		
Decrease	264	-0.006	-0.006	168	-0.008	-0.007
Increase	216	0.000		312	-0.001	
	Livestock heads/ha			Livestock heads/ha		
Decrease	264	0.001	0.005	168	0.008	0.01*
Increase	228	-0.004		324	-0.002	
	Cattle/ha			Cattle/ha		
Decrease	264	0.005	0.007	168	0.008	0.006
Increase	228	-0.002		324	0.002	
	Chickens/ha			Chickens/ha		
Decrease	264	0.034	0.004	168	0.046	0.02
Increase	228	0.030		324	0.025	
	Pigs/ha			Pigs/ha		
Decrease	264	0.002	0.009	168	0.006	0.01
Increase	228	-0.007		324	-0.006	

Notes: Two-tailed t-tests on mean differences of annual growth rates of livestock and crop indicators between the countries that decreased and those that increased N inputs and outputs in the period 2002-14. ***, **, * implies that the difference is different from zero and statistically significant at the 1%, 5% and 10% levels.

Sources: Nitrogen input and output was obtained from OECD (2018[16]) and data on land use and livestock from FAOSTAT (2018[21]).

Similar results are found for changes in P inputs and outputs (Table 3.2). Countries that increased both P inputs and outputs expanded their oil crop cultivation and reduced fruit and vegetable cultivation. They also reduced livestock densities, although the difference is not statistically significant.

Table 3.2. Differences in livestock density and crop mix for countries that increased versus those that decreased P inputs and outputs

Change in input/output	Inputs			Outputs		
	Observations	Mean of annual growth rates	Difference (mean decrease-mean increase)	Observations	Mean of annual growth rates	Difference (mean decrease-mean increase)
Oil crops (ha)				Oil crops (ha)		
Decrease	336	0.027	-0.057***	168	0.013	-0.047***
Increase	144	0.084		312	0.060	
Fruit and vegetables (ha)				Fruit and vegetables (ha)		
Decrease	336	-0.006	0.01**	168	0.002	0.019***
Increase	144	-0.024		312	-0.018	
Cereals (ha)				Cereals (ha)		
Decrease	336	-0.006	-0.008	168	-0.008	-0.007
Increase	144	0.002		312	-0.001	
Livestock heads/ha				Livestock heads/ha		
Decrease	348	0.003	0.005	168	0.007	0.008
Increase	144	-0.002		324	-0.001	
Cattle/ha				Cattle/ha		
Decrease	348	0.006	0.006	168	0.007	0.004
Increase	144	-0.001		324	0.002	
Chickens/ha				Chickens/ha		
Decrease	348	0.037	0.016	168	0.048	0.02
Increase	144	0.021		324	0.024	
Pigs/ha				Pigs/ha		
Decrease	348	-0.004	-0.007	168	0.003	0.01
Increase	144	0.003		324	-0.005	

Notes: This table shows the results of two-tailed t-tests on mean differences of annual growth rates of livestock and crop indicators between countries that decreased and those that increased P inputs and outputs in the period 2002-14. ***, **, * implies that the difference is different from zero and statistically significant at the 1%, 5% and 10% levels.

Sources: Nitrogen input and output was obtained from OECD (2018[16]) and data on land use and livestock from FAOSTAT (2018[21]).

Countries that experienced increases in both N inputs and outputs reduced the area devoted to fruit and vegetables and increased that devoted to oil crops. Considering these patterns can both generate increases in nutrient inputs and outputs, the effect on the balance is unclear. Livestock changes also seem to play an important role in changing nutrient inputs and outputs. A further investigation into the situation in Canada can help to illustrate these developments. Canada is one of the few countries where nutrient surpluses declined despite increases in fertiliser inputs (Figure 3.1 and Figure 3.4).

The evolution of Canada's livestock composition and crop mix since the 1990s illustrates the relevance and complexity of such drivers. Canada's N surplus per hectare grew by an average 8.2% per year in the 1990s, but fell by 0.5% a year in the 2000s, while P surpluses went from an annual growth of 5.3% to an annual reduction of 13.7% over the same period. Most of this decline can be explained by a combination of changes in livestock density, livestock composition, crop mix, and improved cultivars. The number of cattle as a share of the total number of livestock fell 30% between 1992 and 2014, and harvested oil crops as a share of total harvested crops increased 210% over the same period (Figure 3.5). Farmers have also adopted cultivars with more efficient nutrient uptakes, reducing the need for fertiliser while improving yields

(Han et al., 2015[22]; Iqbal et al., 2016[23]; Morrison et al., 2016[24]; De Bruin and Pedersen, 2009[25]). Most of these changes occurred over the last decade; over the 2002-14 period, livestock density decreased on average 1.6% per year, mainly due to a reduction in cattle heads (Figure 3.5).

Figure 3.5. Canada's agricultural sector produces more oil crops and less cattle, 1992-2014

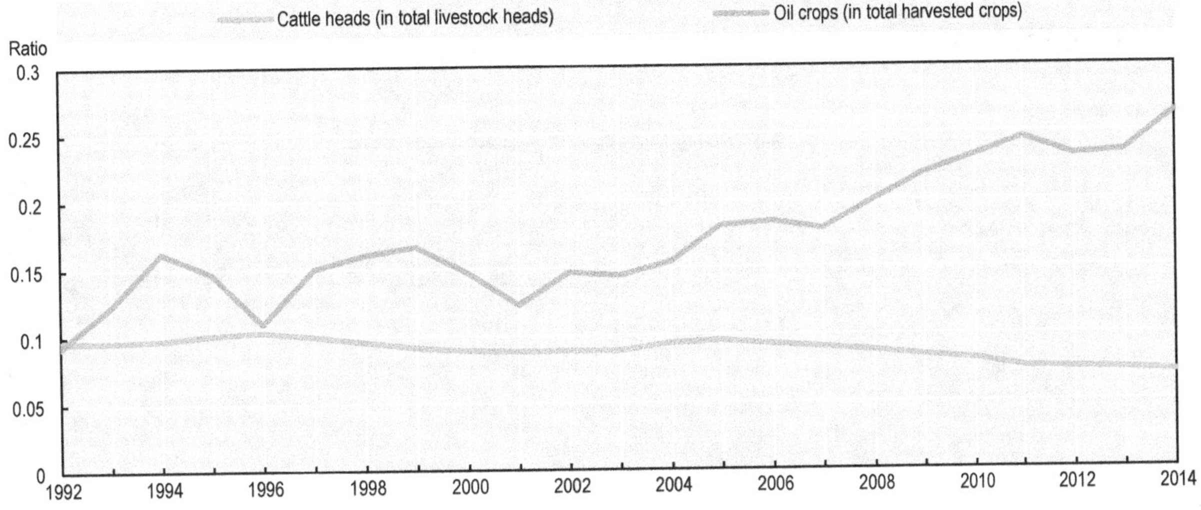

Note: Oil crops and total harvested crops are measured in cultivated hectares.
Source: OECD (2018[16]).

Policy instruments

Agricultural policies can affect environmental outcomes by influencing production patterns, farming practices, and input use (Henderson and Lankoski, 2019[26]). An OECD evaluation of agricultural support policies on the environment found that market price support and payments based on input use appear to consistently increase nitrogen runoff, while payments based on non-current area (cultivated area in previous seasons) and decoupled payments in general seem to have no impact on nutrient balances (Henderson and Lankoski, 2019[26]). As well as general forms of support to agriculture, countries have multiple policies that deal with nutrient surpluses and their impact on water quality, including limits on fertiliser application and livestock density, guidelines for manure application, taxes and subsidies, voluntary schemes, information-based policies, water quality trading, co-operative agreements, and natural-capital-based nutrient allocations (OECD, 2012[27]; OECD, 2017[28]). Countries also have a diverse policy mix in terms of the types of policies they adopt and their geographical scope. This is not surprising considering nutrient pollution sources from agriculture are difficult to identify (nonpoint); a mix of policies and regulatory approaches are often more effective than a single policy at tackling non-point source pollution (OECD, 2010[29]; OECD, 2017[28]).

While there is no "one-size fits all" policy, some attributes of policies can improve the effectiveness of the policy mix, such as monitoring and enforcing the policy, or appropriate targeting (OECD, 2010[29]; OECD, 2017[28]; OECD, 2017[30]). Targeting addresses questions about who and to what degree a regulation should apply. Poorly targeted policy instruments are likely to be ineffective at tackling nutrient balance surpluses, which are mainly generated locally.

An example of a targeted policy is the Nitrate Vulnerable Zones (NVZs) policy mandated by the European Union (EU) Nitrates Directive (OECD, 2017[28]) and, by definition, confined to EU countries. NVZs are those land areas that drain into polluted waters or water sources at risk of nitrate pollution if no action is taken. EU Member States are required to declare NVZs and revise and update them every four years. States that implement a national action program covering all its territory to tackle nitrogen pollution are not required to designate NVZs. Austria, Denmark, Finland, Germany, Ireland, Lithuania, Luxembourg, Malta, the Netherlands, and Slovenia, as well as the region of Flanders and Northern Ireland have implemented action programs. For the rest of EU Member countries, NVZs have been progressively expanded over time and by 2015 covered on average 30% of their respective territories (Figure 3.6). In some cases, however, there have been delays in the implementation of policies (OECD, 2018[31]).

Figure 3.6. Designated nitrate vulnerable zones as submitted by EU Member States

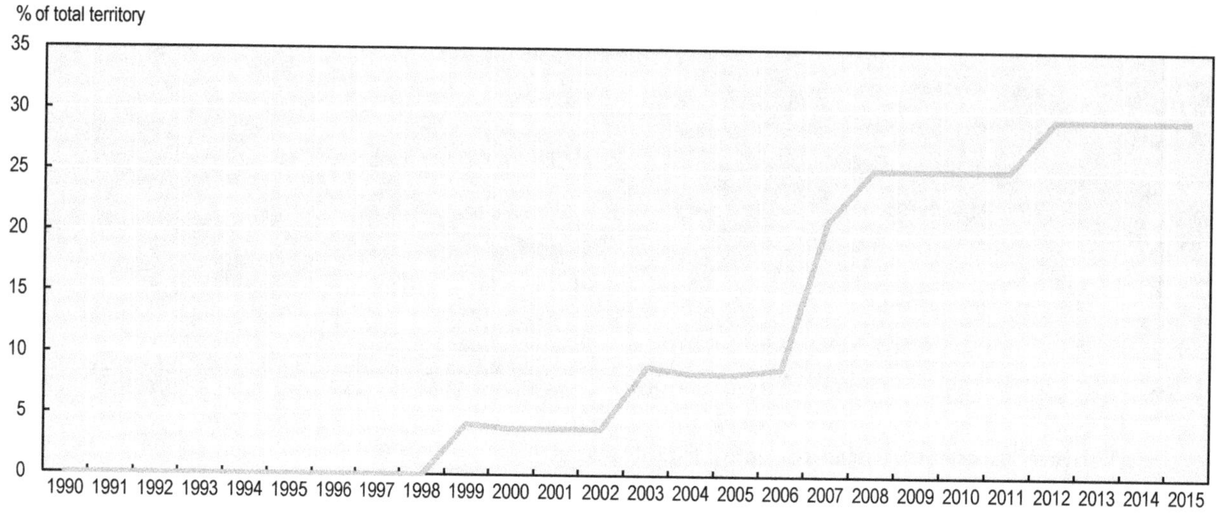

Note: Countries that followed a whole-territory approach to NVZs are excluded from this figure.
Source: (OECD, 2018[31]).

Farmers in NVZs must comply with measures included in the Codes of Good Agricultural Practice. Although each individual EU Member State defines these practices, they must include "measures limiting the periods when nitrogen fertilisers can be applied on land in order to target application to periods when crops require nitrogen and prevent nutrient losses to waters; measures limiting the conditions for fertiliser application (on steeply sloping ground, frozen or snow covered ground, near water courses, etc.) to prevent nitrate losses from leaching and run-off; requirement for a minimum storage capacity for livestock manure; and crop rotations, soil winter cover, and catch crops to prevent nitrate leaching and run-off during wet seasons" (European Commission, 2018[32]). The application of both fertiliser and livestock manure is limited in NVZs; in the case of fertiliser, it is based on crop needs and all N inputs into the soil, while manure is limited to 170 kg nitrogen/hectare/year including both manure spreading and direct application by grazing animals.

In order to empirically relate nutrient balances to agricultural policies (both general and targeted at addressing N pollution), as well as livestock and cropland types, an econometric analysis was carried out to correlate agriculture, economic and policy variables with N and P balances (Table 3.3). The analysis considered two types of policy variables: those specifically addressing nitrogen issues and those affecting all agriculture. Policies directly addressing nutrient pollution are represented by variables that take a value of one for the period when a given country applied a national program to tackle nitrogen pollution "NVZ (whole country)" or a program in a specific territory "NVZ (partial region)". Agriculture support figures were obtained from Anderson and Valenzuela (2008[33]) and are divided into distortionary policies (labelled "coupled support") and decoupled policies (labelled "decoupled payments"). The former include market price support and subsidies linked to input or production, while the latter represent support not linked to current production, inputs or area of production.[1] Livestock and cropland mix variables were included to control for the composition of the sector. To assess the impact of the level of development of a given country, per capita gross domestic product (GDP) was also included as an explanatory variable.

Table 3.3. The role of livestock, crop mix and agricultural policies on nutrient balances

	N per ha		P per ha	
Controls	Model 1	Model 2	Model 1	Model 2
GDP per capita	0.144	0.107	1.176*	0.491
	(0.129)	(0.139)	(0.618)	(0.610)
Nitrate Vulnerable Zone (whole country)	-0.280***	-0.224***	-0.443***	-0.300**
	(0.058)	(0.048)	(0.145)	(0.135)
Nitrate Vulnerable Zone (partial region)	-0.013	0.036	-0.138	0.028
	(0.059)	(0.051)	(0.135)	(0.126)
Coupled support	0.112***	0.078***	0.206***	0.122**
	(0.024)	(0.025)	(0.056)	(0.055)
Decoupled payments	-0.007	0.005	0.015	0.023
	(0.017)	(0.012)	(0.048)	(0.037)
Oil crops (share of cultivated area)		0.133*		0.163
		(0.067)		(0.100)
Cereals (share of cultivated area)		0.174		0.683
		(0.193)		(0.430)
Fruit and Vegetable (share of cultivated area)		-0.124		0.062
		(0.124)		(0.240)
Cattle (heads per hectare)		0.308**		0.354
		(0.139)		(0.329)
Poultry (heads per hectare)		0.080		0.653***
		(0.074)		(0.219)
Pigs (heads per hectare)		0.161		0.356
		(0.102)		(0.260)
Trend	0.004	-0.004	-0.050***	-0.062***
	(0.007)	(0.005)	(0.018)	(0.018)
Year fixed effect	Yes	Yes	Yes	Yes
Country fixed effect	Yes	Yes	Yes	Yes
Observations	566	545	524	504
R-squared	0.332	0.410	0.495	0.554
Number of countries	35	34	34	33

Notes: Coefficients were estimated using a fixed effects model and robust standard errors are presented in parenthesis. *, ** and *** represent statistically significant coefficients at the 10%, 5% and 1% levels, respectively. All variables were transformed to logarithms, except for NVZs, which are dummy variables that take a value of 1 when a given country declared NVZs. Due to data availability for policy variables, the sample covers 1990-2011.
Sources: N and P balances were obtained from the OECD (2018[16]). Coupled and decoupled support variables were obtained from Anderson and Valenzuela (2008[33]), livestock and cropland composition variables were downloaded from FAOSTAT (2018[21]), and GDP per capita from the World Bank Development Indicators Database (World Bank, 2018[34]). NVZs dummies were constructed from the information provided by the Nitrates Directive (European Commission, 2018[32]).

The analysis estimated two econometric models for each nutrient balance: Model 1 includes only economic and policy controls and Model 2 adds livestock and cropland composition explanatory variables. The main results suggest that:

- For countries that declared NVZs, both NVZ variables (whole country and partial regions) are associated with decreased nutrient balances per hectare. However, only the whole-country NVZ approach is statistically significant in both specifications (declaring a whole-country NVZ is associated with a 22% decrease in N balance and a 30% decrease in P balance).[2] Considering only EU countries have NVZ policies, the NVZ finding does not imply that other forms of policy interventions that non-EU countries may have enacted were not effective; to the extent that other countries' N policies are omitted from the analysis, the fact that the NVZ coefficient is statistically significant reflects that NVZ policies tend to stand out compared to other countries' policies.[3] Interestingly, while NVZs mostly target N, they also seem to affect P, possibly to the fact that regulations in NVZs, are also likely to impact P surpluses

- Distortionary forms of agriculture support are positively associated with increases of both surpluses in a statistically significant way (a 1% increase in this form of support is associated with a 0.07% increase in N balance and a 0.12% increase in P balance), decoupled support has no statistically significant association with balances.

- Oil crops are positively associated with N balance and this association is statistically significant at the 10% level: a 1% increase in the oil-crop cultivation area is associated with a 0.13% increase in N balance; while they are also positively associated with P balance, the coefficient is not statistically significant.

- Livestock density, particularly cattle density, has a strong and positive association with N balances (a 1% increase in cattle density is associated with a 0.3% increase in N balance), while poultry density is associated with P balances (a 1% increase in poultry density is associated with a 0.7% increase in P balance). Livestock density is highly associated with the intensification of livestock operations, which has been on the rise globally, contributing to an increase in animal production (Liu et al., 2010[35]). Highly intensive livestock operations rely on concentrated feed and are less dependent on open-range feeding (Bouwman, 2013[7]). While intensive operations tend to lead to more efficient nutrient uptake by individual animals, at the livestock system scale, once the cultivation of feed crops has been taken into account, the efficiency gains from those systems are not clear (Bouwman, 2013[7]). These systems face additional challenges such as the handling of large amounts of manure and, when established in areas with limited amounts of agricultural land, few possibilities for its reuse.

Improved farm management practices

The reduction in P surpluses observed in the majority of OECD countries in the last two decades can be partly associated with higher rates of soil testing in farms (Figure 3.2). Through soil testing in areas such as Western Europe, which have historically had persistently high rates of P applications, farmers have recognised that they can reduce P application rates without compromising yields (Schoumans, 2015[36]).

Soil testing is part of a group of practices branded "improved farm management practices" or "best management practices" (BMPs), which aim to decrease the environmental and health impacts from agricultural activities while maintaining farm productivity. There are a large variety of BMPs, from practices that require significant effort, like introducing conservation tillage and crop rotation, to simple actions like avoiding the application of manure when rain is forecast (Sharpley et al., 2006[37]). Consequently, the economic cost of implementing different BMPs can vary substantially, depending on their scope and complexity. Big structural changes, like implementing manure storage systems, are usually more expensive than more basic measures, such as choosing the right time for manure application (Sharpley et al., 2006[37]); establishing livestock watering systems away from stream corridors can be comparably more costly than creating grass or forest buffers (Shortle et al., 2013[38]). Moreover, the implementation of BMPs will also vary according to the type of farm and the geographic condition where the farm is located (Shortle et al., 2013[38]).

Best management practices for applying fertiliser are usually linked to the 4R Principles: right rate, right timing, right source and right placement. The International Plant Nutrition Institute (2007[39]) summarises these principles as follows:

- *Right rate:* Assess and make decisions based on soil nutrient supply and plant needs.

- *Right timing:* Assess and make decisions based on the dynamics of crop uptake, soil supply, nutrient loss risks and field operation logistics.

- *Right source:* Ensure a balanced supply of essential nutrients, considering both naturally available sources and the characteristics of specific products.

- *Right placement:* Address root-soil dynamics and nutrient movement, and manage spatial variability within the field to meet site-specific crop needs and limit potential losses from the field.

Soil testing is crucial for reducing nutrient application rates and it is directly related to the "right rate" principle. Other BMPs such as conservation tillage, conservation crop rotation and cover crops can also reduce nutrient surpluses (OECD, 2016[40]). Numerous previous studies have found positive impacts from BMPs in reducing nitrate leaching and improving water quality. For instance, pre-sidedress nitrate tests[4] have significantly reduced post-harvest residual soil nitrates (NO_3) in cornfields (Durieux et al., 1995[41]; Justes et al., 2012[42]). Similarly, conservation tillage practices have resulted in reduced NO_3 leaching when compared with conventional tillage (Randall and Iragavarapu, 1995[43]; Weed and Kanwar, 1996[44]). Other studies have shown that the use of cover crops during the inter-growing season has led to lower residual soil NO_3 and reduced leaching in corn and other field crops (McCracken et al., 1994[45]; Mary et al., 1999[46]; Justes et al., 2012[42]). New technologies emerging in the agriculture sector can facilitate BMPs and, therefore, affect nutrient balances (Box 3.1).

Other technological developments include enhanced efficiency N fertilisers (EEFs) which release N at a slower rate than conventional fertilisers or delay the N transformation processes by using inhibitors or coating materials. These can improve crop uptake of N and reduce the risk of N leaching, but their performance depends on the type of crop and the biophysical conditions of the farm, as well on management practices. EEFs can be categorised into four types (Li et al., 2018[47]): 1) urease inhibitors, which delay urea hydrolysis, thus lowering ammonia emission potential; 2) nitrification inhibitors, which reduce the activities of nitrifying bacteria, thereby reducing the risks of nitrate leaching and nitrous oxide emission; 3) double inhibitors, which are designed to lower ammonia, nitrate and nitrous oxides emission losses by combining urease and nitrification inhibitors; and 4) polymer-coated fertilisers, which use partially permeable coating material to control N release. According to a meta-analysis of studies conducted from 1970 to 2016, urease inhibitors and polymer-coated fertilisers were the most effective EEFs for reducing ammonia emissions (Pan et al., 2016[48]). Double inhibitors were most effective in increasing yields and improving nitrogen uptake when applied on grassland, while EEFs were in general less effective in wheat and maize systems (Li et al., 2018[47]). While EEFs can potentially increase yields and reduce environmental risks, their effectiveness is highly dependent on farm management practices (Li et al., 2018[47]).

Box 3.1. The potential impact of precision agriculture on nutrient pollution

Precision agriculture aims to monitor and improve the financial performance of farms at within-field resolution by providing detailed information on site-specific yield, nutrient recovery and income (Wong, M.; Asseng, H.; Zhang, H., 2005[49]). Recovery of nutrients can be used to evaluate and manage environmental risk such as nitrate leaching (Ortega and et al., 2003[50]). Some of the most important groups of technologies used in precision agriculture are:

- *Geographic Information Systems (GIS):* Software to manage spatial data
- *Global Positioning Systems (GPS):* Provides topographical information used by GISs
- *Remote sensors:* Cameras on satellites and airplanes to identify the characteristics of a given area

- *In situ sensors*: Electronic devices to measure soil properties, pests, crop health, etc.
- *Yield monitoring*: Measures the crop yield during harvest, providing a yield map with information on production and variability
- *Variable rate technology*: It applies inputs according to specific needs at a precise location (Joint Research Centre (JRC) of the EC, 2014[51]; OECD, 2016[40]; OECD, 2019[52]).

GIS and GPS technology

Field studies have shown that site-specific in-season adjustments of fertiliser inputs to account for climatic conditions and varying yield potential differences increase fertiliser nitrogen use efficiency up to 368% compared with common farming practices (Diacono, 2013[53]). When sensors are used with GPS, and GIS is used to produce prescription maps (e.g. for guiding variable fertiliser or irrigation applications), the extra cost savings can be over 10-20%, depending on the inherent variability and need for variable inputs in a given field (Diacono, 2013[53]). Research has also shown that the use of GPS ("autosteer") in farm machinery can increase the efficiency of nutrient use by 5-10% (Craighead and Yule, 2001[54]). GPS-based guidance systems with automatic controls allow farmers to precisely apply inputs by both modulating the quantities and by reducing nutrient usage in no-application areas and can therefore generate positive environmental effects (Bongiovanni and Lowenberg-Deboer, 2004[55]).

Variable rate technologies

Thoele and Ehlert (2010[56]) analysed the potential impact of using a mechanical crop biomass sensor ("crop meter"). They found that its use improved N efficiency by 10-15%, and reduced N fertiliser applications without reducing crop yields. Other studies (Anselin, Bongiovanni and Lowenberg-DeBoer, 2004[57]; Meyer-Aurich et al., 2010[58]) concluded that site-specific management of nitrogen fertiliser leads to improvements on N efficiency by 10-15%. Applying at variable rates may not necessarily result in lower fertiliser application rates, however (Dillon and Kusunose, 2013[59]). A similar mixed picture can be found among country experiences with variable rate applications of nitrogen (Lawes, 2011[60]; Boyer et al., 2011[61]; Olesen et al., 2004[62]; Biermacher et al., 2009[63]).

Remote sensors

Mounted in satellites or aircraft, sensors have the potential to produce relevant data for improving the environmental performance of agricultural activities (OECD, 2019[52]). The most relevant applications for agriculture are monitoring crop yield, biomass, crop nutrient and water stress, and detection of pests and soil properties (Mulla, 2013[64]). These technologies have the potential to improve the effectiveness of agri-environmental policies and the quality and scope of agri-environmental indicators (OECD, 2018[16]; OECD, 2019[52]).

3.4. Policy lessons from Korea and Denmark

This section delves further into the role that policies play in decreasing nutrient inputs in soils by describing the approaches of two OECD countries, Korea and Denmark, that best illustrate this.

Korea

Removing some of the most distortionary agricultural subsidies not only creates efficiency gains but can also help reduce environmental pressures. Korea experienced the largest decrease in N fertiliser inputs from 2002 to 2014 in the OECD (Figure 3.7). Decoupling farmers' payments from input use was one of the main reasons behind this change. Nevertheless, Korea still faces significant challenges in dealing with high input levels from manure.

The Korean government has implemented a variety of measures to reduce the overuse of chemical fertilisers. In 1990, it liberalised the sale of agricultural chemicals by progressively reducing domestic subsidies.[5] Although some restrictions on domestic sales of formulated products by foreign companies remained, these were removed at the end of 1999 (OECD, 1999[65]). Since the 2000s, Korea has framed its policies within specific targets. Through the Environmentally Friendly Agriculture Fostering Act, enacted in 1997, the Korean government has established policy plans every five years, starting in 2001, to promote "environmental friendly agriculture". This is defined as a type of agriculture that does not use "chemical materials, such as synthetic agricultural chemicals, chemical fertilisers, antibiotics and antimicrobials, or that minimises the use of such materials, while maintaining and preserving the agricultural ecosystem and environment by recycling by-products of agriculture, fisheries, stock breeding or forestry" (Ministry of Agriculture, Food and Rural Affairs, 2015[66]).

In particular, the plans focus on promoting the safe and appropriate use of agricultural chemicals, setting maximum limits for chemical residues and effluent from livestock excretion, encouraging compliance with fertiliser application rates for each crop, banning the dumping of agricultural waste, and establishing requirements for converting animal excretion into solid and liquid manure. They also define a framework for certifying environmentally friendly agricultural products and establish direct payments to compensate for reduced yields that result from adopting environmentally friendly farming practices (OECD, 2008[67]). For example, a policy objective in the most recent five-year plan (2016-20) is to reduce the quantity of chemical fertilisers and pesticides by 9% relative to 2014 levels.

The Korean government began to decrease subsidies for chemical fertilisers in 1996, and these have now been completely eliminated. This policy change was the main reason for the reduction in chemical fertiliser use over the last decade (Korean Fertilizer Association, 2015[68]), and manure is now the main nutrient input into soils (Figure 3.7).

However, the rapid transformation of the Korean agriculture sector over the last five decades has been driven mainly by new patterns of food consumption: meat consumption increased from 5.2 kg per person in 1970 to 46.8 kg in 2015, and consumption of dairy products increased from 1.6 kg per person in 1970 to 75.7 kg in 2015 (OECD, 2018[69]). As a consequence, the livestock sector experienced the sharpest growth in the country's agriculture sector from 1970 to 2013; the value of livestock products increased from 15% of total agricultural production to 46% over that period (OECD, 2018[69]). To cope with the increasing demand for meat and dairy products, livestock density has increased, leading to greater environmental pressures per unit of land.

While Korea has successfully lowered fertiliser use, mainly by eliminating fertiliser subsidies, manure management remains a challenge. Korea has the largest nitrogen surplus per hectare among OECD countries (Figure 3.2) and the second largest phosphorus surplus per hectare (Figure 3.3). Since the size of the livestock industry keeps growing while the total area of cropland keeps declining, the management of an excess supply of manure is a pressing issue. The Livestock Excretion Management and Use Act passed in 2007 promotes the recycling of manure, mainly to produce and use solid/liquefied fertiliser and energy (Gruère, Ashley and Cadilhon, 2018[70]). While the programme got off to a slow start, chemical fertiliser is increasingly being replaced by recycled manure to deal with the environmental pressures derived from livestock waste.

Figure 3.7. Evolution of nitrogen and phosphorus inputs in Korea, 1985-2015

Kg/ha

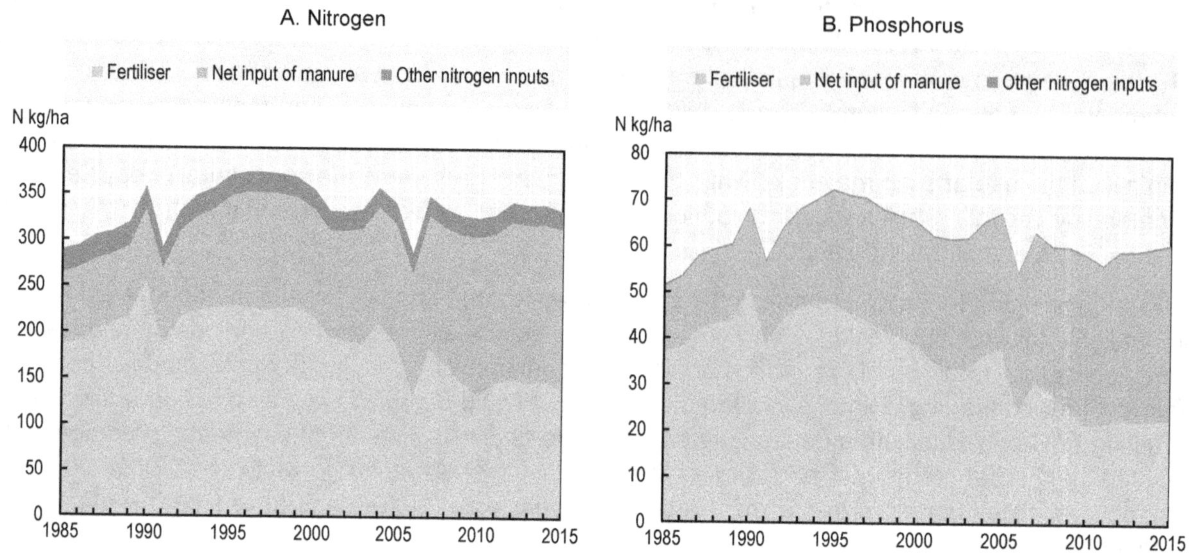

Source: OECD (2018[16]).

Denmark

Acting early, defining clear nutrient pollution reduction targets, constant monitoring and evaluation of policies, and a coherent policy mix can yield sustained reductions in nutrient surpluses while improving the performance of agriculture. Denmark is one of the few OECD countries that has simultaneously experienced an expansion in agricultural production and a decline in nutrient balance surpluses since the 1990s. Underlying this success is a long history of adopting, monitoring and evaluating regulations, as well as combining a wide range of command-and-control, market-based, voluntary, and information regulations.

Denmark's nitrogen and phosphorus balances per hectare have consistently fallen since the 1990s while agricultural production has exhibited steady growth (Figure 3.8). Denmark and the Netherlands are the only OECD countries that have achieved significant nutrient balance reductions and steady agricultural production growth in the last two decades. Moreover, despite having one of the most developed environmental regulation systems in the world (Grinsven et al., 2012[71]), agricultural exports account for more than double its domestic consumption (FAO, 2014[72]) and more than 60% of Denmark's land area is used for agriculture.

Denmark acted early to monitor and combat nitrogen pollution. High nitrogen concentrations were detected in groundwater used for household consumption during the 1980s, and surveys and monitoring of oxygen concentrations in the Danish marine waters indicated an increase in the frequency of oxygen depletion events (Kronvang et al., 2008[73]). Since the early 1980s, multiple regulations have been implemented via the Action Plans for Aquatic Environment (1987, 1998, and 2004), Sustainable Agriculture (1990 and 1996) and Green Growth (2009) policies. The Danish policy mix falls into three categories (Dalgaard et al., 2014[74]): command and control measures, market-based regulations, and information and voluntary action. In particular, the policy mix often includes targets for both reductions of N and P discharges, includes fertiliser accounting systems, N quota systems which regulate the use of fertilisers, bans on manure application on bare fields, fertiliser taxes for non-agricultural uses, taxes on phosphorus content in feed, agri-environmental schemes, and advisory services (OECD, 2018[69]).

Figure 3.8. Agricultural production and nutrient balances in Denmark, 1990-2015

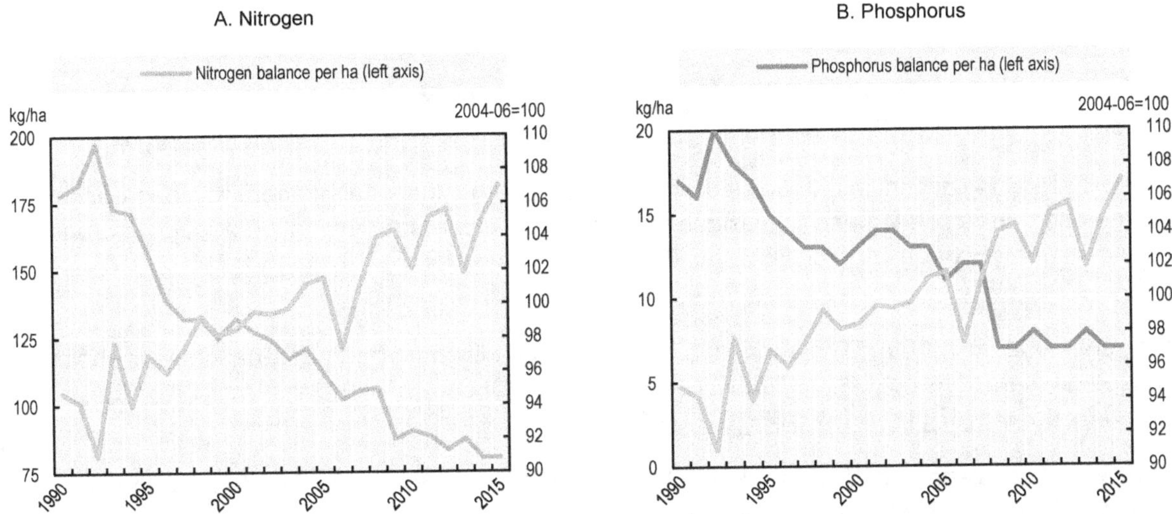

Sources: Nitrogen and phosphorus balance were obtained from OECD (2018[16]); agricultural production index from FAOSTAT (2018[21]).

While Denmark has a multiplicity of regulatory instruments in place, they all contribute to the achievement of clear and well-established targets defined in the action plans. More importantly, even though targets are not always reached, constant monitoring and evaluation of plans and policies have been key to improving the effectiveness of policies (OECD, 2018[69]; Tan and Mudgal, 2013[75]). Since the 1990s, with the implementation of environmentally sensitive areas (ESAs), Denmark has also started to move towards geographically targeted regulations, which tend to be more cost-effective.

Notes

[1] While the OECD Producer Support Estimate database is more accurate and can be divided in different categories of support, it was not possible to use it for this exercise as EU support is reported as an aggregate, so all the variability needed to identify the effects of other policies would have been lost.

[2] The lack of a statistically significant coefficient on NVZ (Partial region) should not be considered as a reason to argue against the effectiveness of the partial territory approach, as it may be explained by the fact that the dependent variable is a crude whole-country measure of the nitrogen balance and it could be masking improvements in specific regions within countries that have declared regional NVZs.

[3] To test the robustness of these findings, the specifications were estimated only for EU countries and the results did not change the main conclusions.

[4] A soil nitrate test used to determine if additional fertiliser nitrogen is needed for corn.

[5] In the case of pesticides, subsidies were supplied through the National Agricultural Co-operatives Federation (NACF). As for fertilisers, from 1982 to 1994, the government subsidised their prices through the Agricultural Chemicals Account (OECD, 1999[65]).

References

Anderson, K. and E. Valenzuela (2008), *Estimates of Global Distortions to Agricultural Incentives, 1955 to 2007*, World Bank, http://dx.doi.org/www.worldbank.org/agdistortions. [33]

Anselin, L., R. Bongiovanni and J. Lowenberg-DeBoer (2004), "A spatial econometric approach to the economics of site-specific nitrogen management in corn production", *American Journal of Agricultural Economics*, Vol. 86/3, pp. 675-687, http://dx.doi.org/10.1111/j.0002-9092.2004.00610.x. [57]

Biermacher, J. et al. (2009), "The economic potential of precision nitrogen application with wheat based on plant sensing", *Agricultural Economics*, Vol. 40, pp. 397–407, http://dx.doi.org/10.1111/j.1574-0862.2009.00387.x. [63]

Billen, G., L. Lassaletta and J. Garnier (2015), "A vast range of opportunities for feeding the world in 2050: Trade-off between diet, N contamination and international trade", *Environmental Research Letters*, Vol. 10/2, http://dx.doi.org/10.1088/1748-9326/10/2/025001. [19]

Bomans E., F. (2005), *Addressing phosphorus related problems in farm practice*, Final report to the European Commission. Soil Service of Belgium. [13]

Bongiovanni, R. and J. Lowenberg-Deboer (2004), "Precision agriculture and sustainability", *Precision Agriculture*, Vol. 5/4, pp. 359-387, http://dx.doi.org/10.1023/B:PRAG.0000040806.39604.aa. [55]

Bouwman, L. (2013), "Exploring global changes in nitrogen and phosphorus cycles in agriculture induced by livestock production over the 1900-2050 period", *PNAS*, Vol. 110/52, pp. 20882-20887. [7]

Boyer, C. et al. (2011), "Profitability of variable rate nitrogen application in wheat production", *Precision Agriculture*, Vol. 12/4, pp. 473-487, https://doi.org/10.1007/s11119-010-9190-5. [61]

Chorus, I. (1999), *Toxic cyanobacteria in water: A guide to their public health consequences, monitoring and management*, E & FN Spon, London. [14]

Conley, D. et al. (2009), "Controlling Eutrophication: Nitrogen and Phosphorus", *Science*, Vol. 323/5917, pp. 1014-1015, http://dx.doi.org/10.1126/science.1167755. [1]

Craighead, M. and I. Yule (2001), "Opportunities for increased profitability from precision agriculture", *Geospatial Information and Agriculture*, http://www.regional.org.au/au/gia/13/439yule.htm. [54]

Dalgaard, T. et al. (2014), "Policies for agricultural nitrogen management—trends, challenges and prospects for improved efficiency in Denmark.", *Environmental Research Letters*, Vol. 9/11, http://dx.doi.org/10.1088/1748-9326/9/11/115002. [74]

De Bruin, J. and P. Pedersen (2009), "Growth, Yield, and Yield Component Changes among Old and New Soybean Cultivars", *Agronomy Journal*, Vol. 101/1, p. 124, http://dx.doi.org/10.2134/agronj2008.0187. [25]

Diacono, M. (2013), "Precision nitrogen management of wheat. A review", *Agronomy for Sustainable Development*, Vol. 33/1, https://doi.org/10.1007/s13593-012-0111-z. [53]

Durieux, R. et al. (1995), "Implications of nitrogen management strategies for nitrate leaching potential: Roles of nitrogen source and fertilizer recommendation system", *Agronomy Journal*, Vol. 87/5, pp. 884-887, http://dx.doi.org/10.2134/agronj1995.00021962008700050017x. [41]

European Commission (2018), *Nitrates Directive*, http://ec.europa.eu/environment/water/water-nitrates/index_en.html. [32]

EUROSTAT (2017), *Agri-environmental indicator - risk of pollution by phosphorus:*, http://ec.europa.eu/eurostat/statistics-explained/index.php/Agri-environmental_indicator_-_risk_of_pollution_by_phosphorus#cite_note-6. [12]

FAO (2014), *The State of Food and Agriculture*, FAO publications, Rome. [72]

FAOSTAT (2018), *Food and agriculture data*, http://www.fao.org/faostat/en/#home. [21]

Goulding, K. (2016), "Soil acidification and the importance of liming agricultural soils with particular reference to the United Kingdom", *Soil Use and Management*, Vol. 32/3, pp. 390–399, https://doi.org/10.1111/sum.12270. [10]

Grinsven, V. et al. (2012), "Management, regulation and environmental impacts of nitrogen fertilization in northwestern Europe under the Nitrates Directive: a benchmark study", *Biogeosciences, 9(12), 5143-5160.*, Vol. 9/12, pp. 5143-5160, https://doi.org/10.5194/bg-9-5143-2012. [71]

Gruère, G., C. Ashley and J. Cadilhon (2018), "Reforming water policies in agriculture: lessons from past reforms", *OECD Food, Agriculture and Fisheries Papers* 113, https://doi.org/10.1787/1826beee-en. [70]

Han, M. et al. (2015), "The Genetics of Nitrogen Use Efficiency in Crop Plants", *Annual Review of Genetics*, Vol. 49/1, pp. 269-289, http://dx.doi.org/10.1146/annurev-genet-112414-055037. [22]

Henderson, B. and J. Lankoski (2019), "Evaluating the environmental impact of agricultural policies", *OECD Food, Agriculture and Fisheries Papers*, No. 130, OECD Publishing, Paris, https://dx.doi.org/10.1787/add0f27c-en. [26]

Hitzfeld, B. (2000), "Cyanobacterial Toxins: Removal during Drinking Water Treatment, and Human Risk Assessment", *Environ Health Perspect*, Vol. 1/1, pp. 8113–122, https://doi.org/10.2307/3454636. [15]

International Plant Nutrition Institute (2007), *Right product, right rate, right time and right place… the foundation of best management practices for fertilizer*, http://www.ipni.net/publication/bettercrops.nsf/0/91607AF3210A609F852579800080C01C/$FILE/Better%20Crops%202007-4%20p14.pdf. [39]

Iqbal, M. et al. (2016), "Genetic Improvement in Grain Yield and other Traits of Wheat Grown in Western Canada", *Crop Science*, Vol. 56/2, p. 613, http://dx.doi.org/10.2135/cropsci2015.06.0348. [23]

J.V., S. (ed.) (2013), *Dispelling misperceptions regarding variable rate application*, Wageningen Academic Publishers, https://doi.org/10.3920/978-90-8686-778-3_95. [59]

Joint Research Centre (JRC) of the EC (2014), *Precision Agriculture: An Opportunity for EU farmers- Potential support with the CAP 2014-2020*, https://www.europarl.europa.eu/RegData/etudes/note/join/2014/529049/IPOL-AGRI_NT%282014%29529049_EN.pdf. [51]

Justes, E. et al. (2012), *Réduire les fuites de Nitrate au moyen de cultures intermédiaires*, https://oatao.univ-toulouse.fr/16383/11/Justes_16383.pdf. [42]

Korean Fertilizer Association (2015), *Statistical Yearbook of Fertiliser*. [68]

Kronvang, B. et al. (2008), "Effects of policy measures implemented in Denmark on nitrogen pollution of the aquatic environment", *Environmental Science & Policy*, Vol. 11/2, pp. 144-152, https://doi.org/10.1016/j.envsci.2007.10.007. [73]

Lawes, R. (2011), "Whole farm implications on the application of variable rate technology to every cropped field", *Field Crops Research*, Vol. 124/2, pp. 142-48, https://doi.org/10.1016/j.fcr.2011.01.002. [60]

Li, T. et al. (2018), "Enhanced-efficiency fertilizers are not a panacea for resolving the nitrogen problem", *Global Change Biology*, http://dx.doi.org/10.1111/gcb.13918. [47]

Liu, J. et al. (2010), "A high-resolution assessment on global nitrogen flows in cropland", *PNAS*, Vol. 107/17, pp. 8035-8040, https://doi.org/10.1073/pnas.0913658107. [6]

Liu, J. et al. (2010), "A high-resolution assessment on global nitrogen flows in cropland", *PNAS*, Vol. 107/17, pp. 8035–8040. [35]

Mary, B. et al. (1999), "Calculation of nitrogen mineralization and leaching in fallow soil using a simple dynamic model", *European journal of soil science*, Vol. 50/4, pp. 549-566, https://doi.org/10.1046/j.1365-2389.1999.00264.x. [46]

McCracken, D. et al. (1994), "Nitrate leaching as influenced by cover cropping and nitrogen source", *Soil Science Society of America Journal*, Vol. 58/5, pp. 1476-1483, http://dx.doi.org/10.2136/sssaj1994.03615995005800050029x. [45]

Meyer-Aurich, A. et al. (2010), "Optimal site-specific fertilization and harvesting strategies with respect to crop yield and quality response to nitrogen", *Agricultural Systems*, Vol. 103/7, pp. 478-485, http://dx.doi.org/10.1016/j.agsy.2010.05.001. [58]

Ministry of Agriculture, Food and Rural Affairs (2015), *Act on the promotion of environment-friendly agriculture and fisheries and the management of and support for organic foods*, http://elaw.klri.re.kr. [66]

Morrison, M. et al. (2016), "Canola yield improvement on the Canadian Prairies from 2000 to 2013", *Crop and Pasture Science*, Vol. 67/4, p. 245, http://dx.doi.org/10.1071/CP15348. [24]

Mosier, A. and J. Freney (eds.) (2004), *"Integrated nitrogeninput systems in Denmark"*. [62]

Mosier, A. et al. (1998), "Closing the global N2O budget : nitrous oxide emissions through the agricultural nitrogen cycle inventory methodology", *Nutrient Cycling in Agroecosystems*, Vol. 52/2–3, pp. 225–248, https://doi.org/10.1023/A:1009740530221. [9]

Mulla, D. (2013), "Twenty five years of remote sensing in precision agriculture: Key advances and remaining knowledge gaps", *Biosystems Engineering*, http://dx.doi.org/10.1016/j.biosystemseng.2012.08.009. [64]

OECD (2019), *Digital Opportunities for Better Agricultural Policies*, OECD Publishing, Paris, https://dx.doi.org/10.1787/571a0812-en. [52]

OECD (2018), *Agri-environmental indicators*, http://dx.doi.org/www.oecd.org/agriculture/sustainable-agriculture/agri-environmentalindicators.htm. [16]

OECD (2018), *Agri-environmental indicators*, http://www.oecd.org/tad/sustainable-agriculture/agri-environmentalindicators.htm. [31]

OECD (2018), *Innovation, Agricultural Productivity and Sustainability in Korea*, OECD Food and Agricultural Reviews, OECD Publishing, Paris, https://dx.doi.org/10.1787/9789264307773-en. [69]

OECD (2017), *Diffuse Pollution, Degraded Waters: Emerging Policy Solutions*, OECD Studies on Water, OECD Publishing, Paris, http://dx.doi.org/10.1787/9789264269064-en. [28]

OECD (2017), *Water Risk Hotspots for Agriculture*, OECD Studies on Water, OECD Publishing, Paris, http://dx.doi.org/10.1787/9789264279551-en. [30]

OECD (2016), *Farm Management Practices to Foster Green Growth*, OECD Publishing, Paris, https://doi.org/10.1787/22229523. [40]

OECD (2013), *OECD Compendium of Agri-environmental Indicators*, OECD Publishing, Paris, http://dx.doi.org/10.1787/9789264186217-en. [2]

OECD (2012), *Water Quality and Agriculture: Meeting the Challenge*, OECD Studies on Water, OECD Publishing, http://dx.doi.org/10.1787/22245081. [27]

OECD (2010), *Guidelines for Cost-effective Agri-environmental Policy Measures*, OECD Publishing, Paris, http://dx.doi.org/10.1787/9789264086845-en. [29]

OECD (2008), *Environmental Performance of Agriculture in OECD Countries Since 1990*, OECD Publishing, Paris, http://dx.doi.org/10.1787/9789264040854-en. [3]

OECD (2008), *Evaluation of Agricultural Policy Reforms in Korea*, OECD, Paris, http://www.oecd.org (accessed on 26 February 2018). [67]

OECD (1999), *Review of Agricultural Policies: Korea 1999: National Policies and Agricultural Trade*, OECD Publishing, Paris., http://dx.doi.org/10.1787/9789264172623-en. [65]

OECD/EUROSTAT (2012), *OECD/EUROSTAT Nitrogen Balance Handbook*, OECD Publishing. [4]

OECD/EUROSTAT (2012), *OECD/EUROSTAT Phosphorus Balance Handbook*, OECD Publishing. [5]

Ortega, R. and et al. (2003), *patial variability of wine grape yield and quality in Chilean vineyards: Economic and environmental impacts*. [50]

Pan, B. et al. (2016), "Ammonia volatilization from synthetic fertilizers and its mitigation strategies: A global synthesis", *Agriculture, Ecosystems and Environment*, http://dx.doi.org/10.1016/j.agee.2016.08.019. [48]

Randall, G. and T. Iragavarapu (1995), "Impact of long-term tillage systems for continuous corn on nitrate leaching to tile drainage.", *Journal of Environmental Quality*, Vol. 24/2, pp. 360-366, http://dx.doi.org/10.2134/jeq1995.00472425002400020020x. [43]

Roberts, T. (2015), "Phosphorus use efficiency and management in agriculture", *Resources, Conservation and Recycling*, Vol. 105, pp. 275–281, https://doi.org/10.1016/j.resconrec.2015.09.013. [11]

Schoumans, O. (2015), "Phosphorus management in Europe in a changing world", *Ambio*, Vol. 44/2, pp. S180-92, https://doi.org/10.1007/s13280-014-0613-9. [36]

Sebek, L. et al. (2014), *Nitrogen and phosphorous excretion factors of livestock*, Livestock Research, Wageningen University. [17]

Sebilo, M. (2013), "Long-term fate of nitrate fertilizer in agricultural soils", *PNAS*, Vol. 110/45, pp. 18185-9, https://doi.org/10.1073/pnas.1305372110. [8]

Sharpley, A. et al. (2006), *Best Management Practices To Minimize Agricultural Phosphorus Impacts on Water Quality*, United States Department of Agriculture, ARS-163(July). [37]

Shortle, J. et al. (2013), *Building Capacity to Analyze the Economic Impacts of Nutrient Trading and Other Policy Approaches for Reducing Agriculture's Nutrient Discharge into the Chesapeake Bay Watershed Executive Summary*, USDA, https://www.usda.gov/oce/environmental_markets/files/EconomicTradingCBay.pdf (accessed on 15 May 2018). [38]

Tan, A. and S. Mudgal (2013), *DYNAMIX policy mix evaluation Reducing fertiliser use in Denmark*, http://dynamix-project.eu/sites/default/files/Fertilisers_Denmark.pdf. [75]

Thoele, H. and D. Ehlert (2010), "Biomass Related Nitrogen Fertilization with a Crop Sensor", *Applied Engineering in Agriculture*, Vol. 26/5, http://dx.doi.org/10.13031/2013.34937. [56]

Velthof, G., Y. Hou and O. Oenema (2015), "Nitrogen excretion factors of livestock in the European Union: A review", *Journal of the Science of Food and Agriculture*, https://doi.org/10.1002/jsfa.7248. [18]

Weed, D. and R. Kanwar (1996), "Nitrate and water present in and flowing from root-zone soil", *Journal of Environmental Quality*, Vol. 25/4, pp. 709-719, http://dx.doi.org/10.2134/jeq1996.00472425002500040010x. [44]

Wong, M.; Asseng, H.; Zhang, H. (2005), *Precision agriculture improves efficiency of nitrogen use and minimises its leaching at within-field to farm scales.", In 5th European Conference on Precision Agriculture*. [49]

World Bank (2018), *World Development Indicators*, http://datatopics.worldbank.org/world-development-indicators/. [34]

Zhang, X. et al. (2015), "Managing nitrogen for sustainable development", *Nature*, Vol. 528/7580, pp. 51-59, http://dx.doi.org/doi:10.1038/nature15743. [20]

Annex 3.A. Nutrient balance indicators

Nutrient balance indicators can act as a signal for the potential environmental impact of agriculture on water and air. The OECD agricultural nutrient balance indicators are gross balances. They are calculated at the national level, and measure the difference between the total quantity of nutrient inputs entering an agricultural system (mainly fertilisers and livestock manure), and the quantity of nutrient outputs leaving the system (mainly the uptake of nutrients by crops and grassland) (OECD/EUROSTAT, 2012[4]; OECD/EUROSTAT, 2012[5]). In the case of nitrogen, the gross nutrient balance includes all emissions of environmentally harmful nitrogen compounds from agriculture into the soil, water and the air, while the net balance excludes air emissions (OECD/EUROSTAT, 2012[4]). In the case of phosphorus, there are no air emissions so the gross balance is the same as the net balance (Figure 3.A.1).

Gross balances are expressed in kilogrammes of nutrient surplus per hectare of agricultural land per annum. It is important to bear in mind that these indicators are proxies for environmental pressures at the national level, and do not consider sub-national differences. There are several limitations that could limit cross-country comparisons of nutrient balance levels such as the precision and accuracy of the underlying nutrient conversion factors and the uncertainties involved in estimating nutrient uptake by pasture areas and some fodder crops (OECD, 2013[2]).

Annex Figure 3.A.1. Main components of the gross nitrogen and phosphorus balance calculation

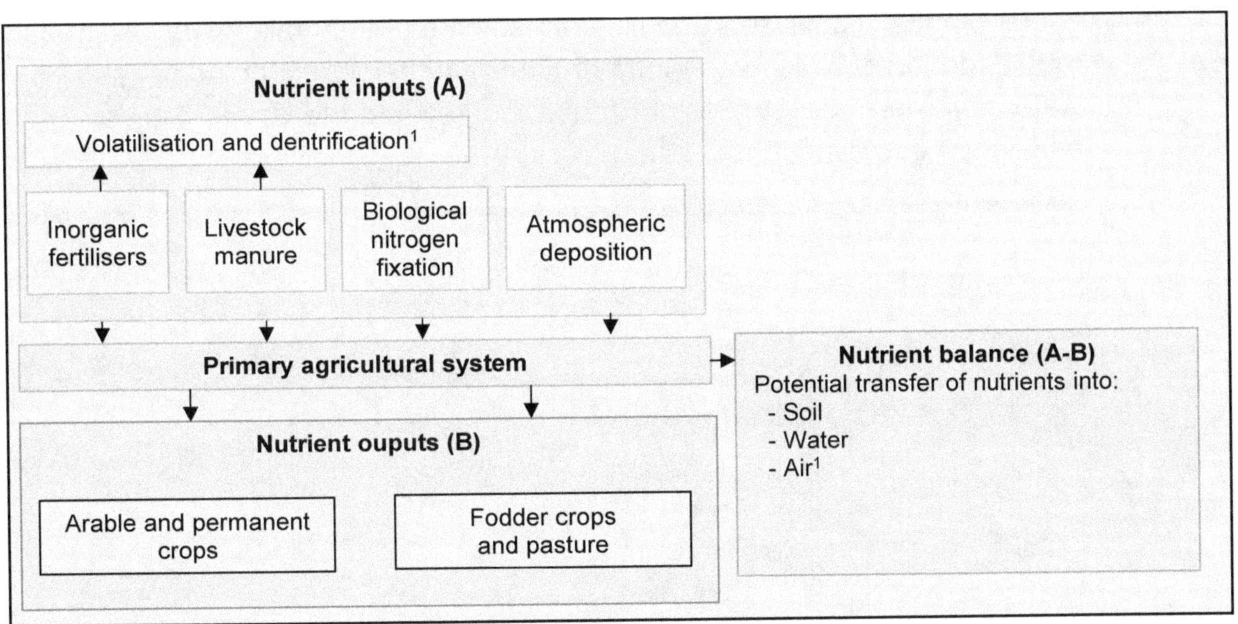

Note: 1. Applies to nitrogen balance only.
Source: (OECD, 2018[16]).

4. Water use and irrigation in agriculture

This chapter reports recent trends in water use indicators in the agricultural sector of OECD countries and illustrates some of the main drivers such as market developments, water infrastructure, irrigation technologies, and water policies. Case studies of France, Turkey and the United States highlight the relevance of these drivers

The statistical data for Israel are supplied by and under the responsibility of the relevant Israeli authorities. The use of such data by the OECD is without prejudice to the status of the Golan Heights, East Jerusalem and Israeli settlements in the West Bank under the terms of international law.

Key messages

- Agricultural water abstraction has decreased in most OECD countries since 2005, confirming a trend observed since the early 2000s. This trend is particularly evident in countries where the irrigation sector is large relative to the agriculture sector. For some countries, the decrease is significant and often associated with deep policy reforms (e.g. in agriculture and water regulation) and the capacity of farmers to adapt to new climate and policy environments. The decrease in water use for irrigation explains most of the decreasing trends of agricultural water use in OECD countries.

- As agriculture accounts for a large proportion of total water use, reductions in water abstraction contributed significantly to lowering total water abstraction in most OECD countries. These reductions have also contributed to the observed decrease in water stress in a majority of OECD countries, especially those with high initial levels of water stress.

- A few OECD countries, such as Mexico and Turkey, continue to expand irrigation, contributing to increased water stress. When expansion of irrigation areas are coupled with more efficient irrigation techniques, water use efficiency improves. Nevertheless, the expansion of the irrigation sector may have led to the observed increase in water stress since 2005 in these countries.

- Many OECD countries rely increasingly on ground rather than surface water for agriculture use, confirming a trend observed since the mid-1990s. Such reliance raises serious sustainability issues because in certain regions these withdrawals exceed the recharge rates, leading to a drop in water tables with potentially negative impacts on the environment and on the future resilience of such production systems. In addition, the environmental impact of groundwater irrigation is generally long lasting, if not irremediable.

- Water application rates (e.g. quantity of irrigation water) have decreased in OECD countries having large irrigation sectors. This suggests significant gains in water use efficiency and changes in crop mixes towards less water-intensive crops.

- The country focus on France, the United States and Turkey illustrates that the irrigation sector appears to adjust to evolving policy, market and climatic conditions.

- In view of the projected increases in drought and flood risks, improving the monitoring of water and the availability and reliability of water statistics is necessary to formulate sound water management policies.

4.1. Water resources in agriculture

Water management is a major political issue in many countries and agriculture plays a fundamental role in this area. Population growth, urbanisation and rising demand for food will increase pressure on water resources. Yet the availability of water resources is increasingly at risk due to climate change, which in turn has resulted in a rising frequency of extreme water events such as droughts and floods. Agriculture is affected by these events because it relies heavily on water and, in most countries, constitutes the largest sector in terms of water use.

To tackle these challenges, management policy of water resources must address the trade-offs between economic, social, and environmental goals, using a combination of regulatory and economic incentives. All OECD countries have developed institutions and laws governing water access, allocation and pricing, as well as a set of policy strategies and instruments to address broad water management goals covering water resources, its quality, and ecosystems protection. In terms of the more specific objectives to manage water resources in agriculture, OECD countries largely share a common strategic vision to (OECD, 2010[1]):

- "establish a long term plan for the sustainable management of water resources in agriculture taking into account climate change impacts, including protection from flood and drought risks;
- contribute to raising agricultural incomes and achieving broader rural development goals;
- protect ecosystems on agricultural land or those affected by farming activities;
- balance agricultural water withdrawals with environmental needs, especially by maintaining minimum flow levels in rivers and lakes and ensuring sustainable use of groundwater resources (i.e. both shallow wells and deep aquifers); and
- improve the efficiency of water resource withdrawal, management, technologies and ensure the financing to maintain and upgrade the infrastructure supplying water to farms (and other water consumers)."

Agricultural water resource management covers a wide range of agricultural systems and climatic conditions across OECD countries. In many countries, rain-fed agriculture dominates, but in areas susceptible to variable precipitation or having water deficits, irrigation is used to supplement periodic shortfalls. In arid areas, crop production may be largely dependent on irrigation.[1] Irrigation water draws mainly on fresh surface water and groundwater, and to a lesser extent on recycled wastewater and desalinated water. The proportions by which these water sources are used vary across countries. Water resource management in agriculture also operates in a highly diverse set of political, cultural, legal and institutional contexts, encompassing a wide range of public policy domains: agriculture, water, environment, energy, fiscal, economic, social, and regional.

4.2. Trends in water use and irrigation indicators

This section describes the trends in the main indicators related to water use in agriculture. Annex 4.A. describes the indicators used.

The degree of water stress, an indicator reflecting water resources availability, varies a great deal among OECD countries from very low (e.g. Canada, Latvia, New Zealand, Slovak Republic, Sweden) to high levels (e.g. Israel, Italy, Korea, Spain, Belgium), reflecting the diversity of conditions in terms of water withdrawals and resources in the OECD area (Figure 4.1). National water stress refers to the indicator intensity of freshwater use, which is measured as the ratio of total freshwater abstractions (all sectors included) to total renewable water resources in the country. A ratio below 10% is typically considered to be low water stress; moderate when between 10% and 20%; medium-high when between 20% and 40%; and high when above 40%.

The water stress indicator has trended slightly downwards in the majority of OECD countries since 2005 due to reductions in total water abstraction. Decreases in water stress are more notable for several countries with medium and high initial levels of water stress – Israel (7 percentage points), Korea (1 percentage points), Belgium (2 percentage points) (Figure 4.1) – and for countries with moderate water stress such as France and Germany (both 2 percentage points). However, water stress increased in some OECD countries facing medium water stress levels such as Turkey (from 19% in 2005 to 22% in 2013), Mexico (from 16% to 18%), and the United States (from 19% to 20%). The OECD average shows stable to slightly increasing water stress, due to the importance of the latter countries in total water abstraction.

Figure 4.1. Water stress decreased slightly in most OECD countries since 2005

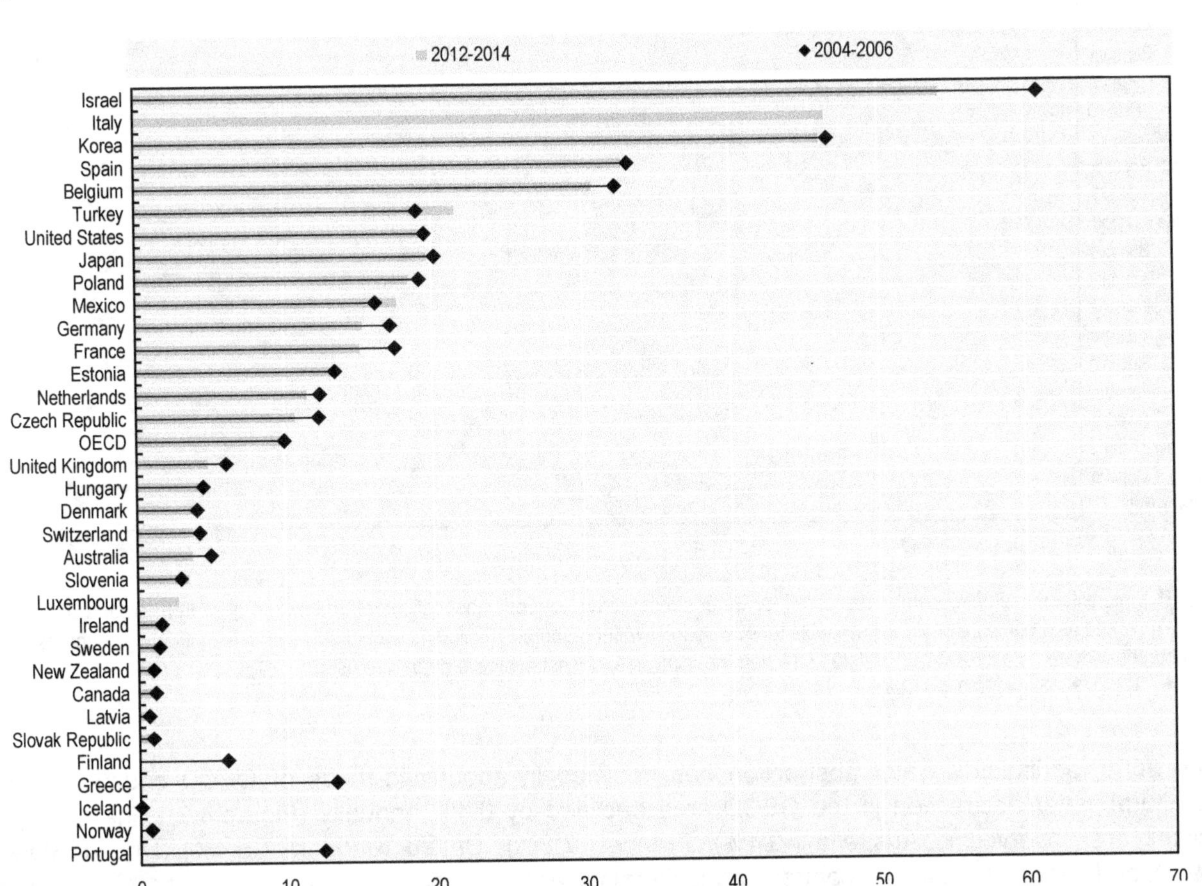

Notes: The intensity of use of freshwater resources (or water stress) refers to gross abstractions of freshwater taken from ground or surface waters expressed as a percentage of total available renewable freshwater resources (including water inflows from neighbouring countries). For some countries, when data for 2004-06 and 2012-14 were not available, closest available data were used.
Sources: (OECD, 2016[2]; OECD, 2016[3]).

Agriculture significantly contributes to national water stress in several OECD countries, particularly those with a relatively large irrigated sector (Figure 4.2). The relatively large weight of agriculture on water stress in OECD countries reflects the important contribution of agriculture on total water abstraction and the role of the irrigation sector. Interestingly, the weight of agriculture in water stress tends to be high in countries having high levels of water stress (e.g. Israel, Italy,[2] Korea, Spain, Turkey, Japan, and Mexico).

Figure 4.2. Agriculture plays a major role in water stress in several OECD countries, 2012-14

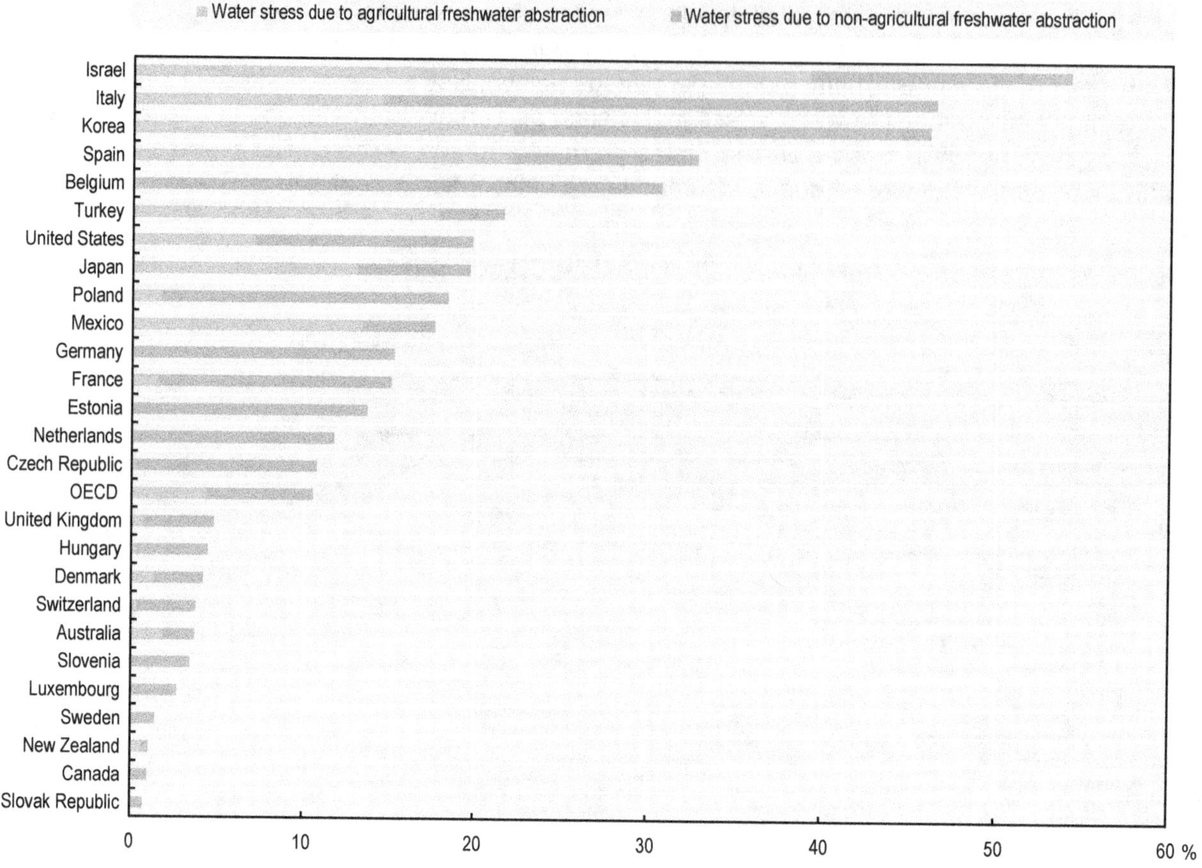

Notes: The intensity of use of freshwater resources (or water stress) refers to gross abstractions of freshwater taken from ground or surface waters expressed as a percentage of total available renewable freshwater resources (including water inflows from neighbouring countries). For some countries where data for 2004-06 and 2012-14 were not available, closest available data were used.
Sources: (OECD, 2016[2]; OECD, 2016[3]).

Since 2005, agricultural water abstraction has declined in about two-thirds of OECD countries, and agricultural water abstraction in the OECD area declined by 0.4% annually (Figure 4.3). The stronger declines are observed in Australia (-9.4%), France (-7.8%), United Kingdom (-5.4%), United States (-1.9%), and Greece (-1.4%). By contrast, agricultural water abstraction increased by about 1% or more in New Zealand, Turkey and Mexico, while countries such as Germany and the Czech Republic had large increases, 13.6% and 8.5%, respectively. Overall, reductions of agricultural water use contributed to reduce water stress; agriculture freshwater abstractions accounted for 42% of total freshwater abstractions in the OECD area in 2012-14, against 43% in 2004-06.

Figure 4.3. Trends in agricultural freshwater abstraction in OECD countries since 2005

Average annual percentage change between 2005 and most recent available year

Average annual percentage change	Average (million m^3)	
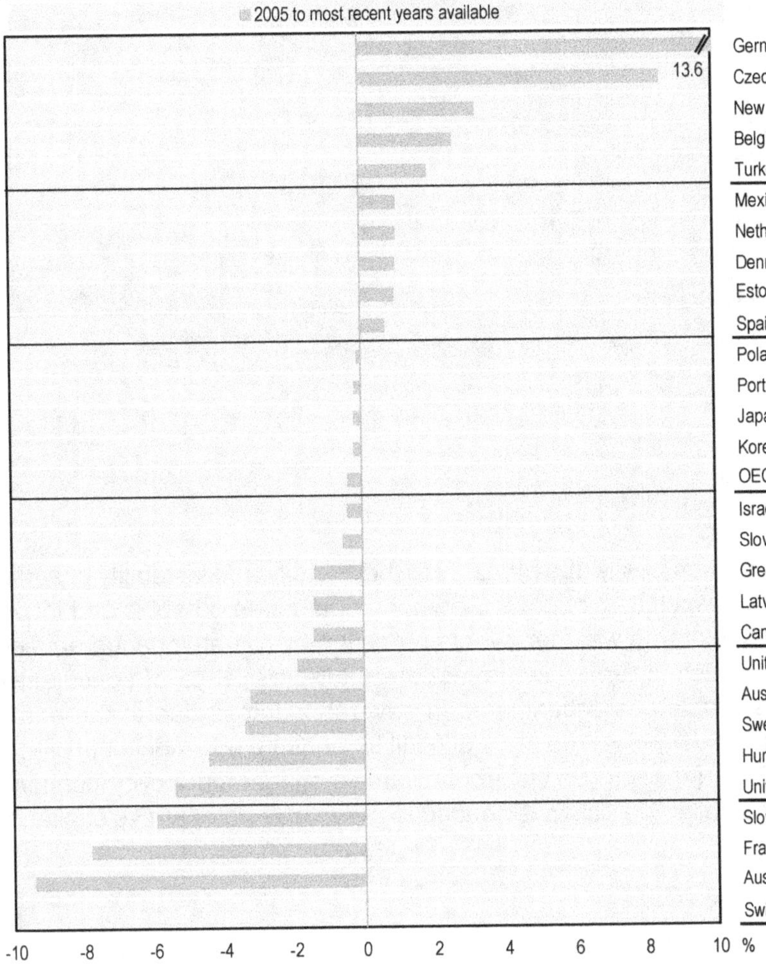 2005 to most recent years available	2004-2006	2012-2014
Germany	132	249
Czech Republic	23	45
New Zealand	2 820	3 207
Belgium	36	39
Turkey	36 749	41 893
Mexico	58 528	63 442
Netherlands	95	100
Denmark	202	219
Estonia [1]	4	5
Spain	23 484	24 441
Poland	1 089	1 080
Portugal	3 437	3 412
Japan	54 963	54 418
Korea	16000	15 900
OECD [2]	419 720	406 695
Israel	1 121	1 107
Slovak Republic	28	27
Greece	8 592	7 918
Latvia	50	46
Canada	2 076	1 908
United States	192 485	175 234
Austria	100	77
Sweden	116	98
Hungary	406	310
United Kingdom	1 498	1 075
Slovenia	4	3
France	4 867	2 994
Australia [3]	10 814	7 290
Switzerland	..	160

(Germany bar: 13.6)

Horizontal axis: -10, -8, -6, -4, -2, 0, 2, 4, 6, 8, 10 %

Notes:
1. For Estonia, data represent water use in agriculture.
2. The OECD total does not include Switzerland in the average annual percentage change.
3. For Australia, 2004-06 is replaced by 2005-06 and 2012-14 by 2009-11.
Sources: (OECD, 2016[2]; OECD, 2016[3]).

While agricultural water use is decreasing, the share of agricultural water abstraction from groundwater continues to increase in several OECD countries (Figure 4.4), particularly in France, Germany, Greece, and the Netherlands. In many areas, recharge rates of groundwater resources are lower than abstraction rates, endangering the sustainability of this resource in the medium and long run. In addition, irrigation not only impacts the availability of water via withdrawals, but can also affect water quality (e.g. salinisation and land subsidence). The sustainability of water use is a particularly significant issue in the case of fossil aquifers, which are not renewable.

Figure 4.4. Groundwater as a share of total agriculture water abstraction

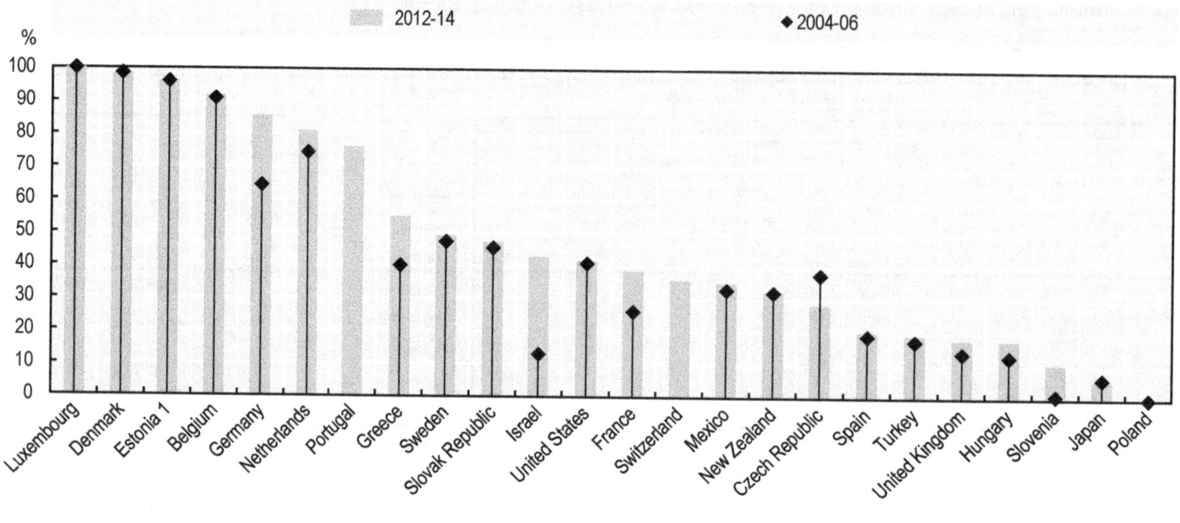

Note: For Estonia, data represent water use in agriculture.
Sources: (OECD, 2016[2]; OECD, 2016[3]).

This increasing pressure on groundwater resources is due primarily to the scarcity and instability of surface water resources. In the longer term, factors such as higher food demand due to demographic and income growth, as well as a higher occurrence of extreme weather events propelled by climate change are likely to put more pressure on this resource, which in turn would affect the future resilience of agriculture to respond to water-supply shortfalls. This problem is accentuated in several countries due to the relative weakness of groundwater regulations; groundwater is also more difficult to measure and monitor in practice than surface water. As indicated in OECD (2015[4]), better groundwater management policy combining regulatory instruments and economic and collective action is needed to overcome water stress challenges in agriculture.

4.3. Drivers of water use and irrigation indicators

Agricultural water abstraction is decreasing due to a decline in irrigated land area, improvements in water use efficiency, and changes in crop mixes

Trends in agricultural water abstraction have several possible causes and reflect different phenomena among OECD countries. Before considering the more fundamental drivers of change (e.g. commodity prices, agricultural policies, environmental regulations, and climate change), an intermediate but necessary first step is to break down the changes in agricultural water abstraction into main drivers. In practice, changes in agricultural water abstraction are the result of a combination of factors such as: i) changes in irrigated areas; ii) changes in crop mix with different water needs; iii) variation of meteorological factors; iv) improvements in water use efficiency; and v) availability, state and management of water storage resources, including changes in water abstraction charges (Box 4.1).

Breaking down the changes in agricultural water abstraction is useful for policy analysis and guidance, but lack of data continues to be a concern for policy assessment. For example, a reduction in agricultural water use in a given country can be due to either improvement of water use efficiency (through modernised irrigation techniques) or to a change in the crop mix, or a combination of the two. These very different situations would need different responses from policy makers.

> **Box 4.1. Breaking down changes in agricultural water abstraction**
>
> *Size effect*: *Ceteris paribus*, trends in agricultural water abstractions can reflect changes in the size of either the agricultural or irrigation sector (irrigated land areas).
>
> *Composition effect*: *Ceteris paribus*, variations can be due to changes in the relative shares of agricultural activities or crops that differ in their water needs. For example, substituting irrigated agriculture by livestock farming can lead to a reduction in total agricultural water abstraction. Changes in the crop mix can also affect agricultural water abstraction due to different crop water needs (e.g. corn is usually more water demanding than beans).
>
> *Meteorological effect*: Depending on the country context, irrigation water abstractions can be complementary to net precipitation; in these cases irrigation water abstractions are generally negatively correlated with net precipitation. More precipitation can reduce both water use per hectare within the growing season and the area devoted to irrigation. In arid regions, irrigation is the major source of water for crop needs, and so less likely to vary negatively with net precipitation.
>
> *Water use efficiency effect*: Improvements in water use efficiency due to, for example, upgrades of irrigation material (reducing water leakages) or better management through more advanced use of weather information systems can explain some variations in agricultural water abstraction.
>
> *Water resource effect*: Accessibility of water resources via wells, dams and other forms of water infrastructure play a critical role in farmers' decision to irrigate. This effect relates to meteorological conditions, since water resources typically depend on cumulative precipitation over a certain period of time (e.g. recharge of dams during the winter season), but also on the water storage infrastructure and its management.

Irrigation is a driving force of agricultural water use in most OECD countries, accounting for more than 60% of agricultural water use in most OECD countries, and over 90% in countries such as France, Israel, Mexico, Spain, Turkey, and the United States (Figure 4.5). In countries with less or no irrigation, agriculture water abstraction is mainly used for livestock. Irrigation intensity (ratio of irrigated area to cropping area) is typically high in southern Europe, but also in countries such as the United Kingdom, Denmark, and the Netherlands (BIO Intelligence Service, 2012[5]).

Trends in agricultural water abstraction closely follow those of irrigation water use, implying that irrigation plays an important role in OECD countries in sustainable water resource management. Where there is a large irrigation sector, irrigation water use dictates the overall trend. However, even in countries with relatively small irrigation sectors, irrigation water abstraction tends to decrease in conjunction with other forms of agricultural water uses (e.g. livestock) and closely follow the same trends. This indicates that water use in the livestock sector has experienced significant reductions.

Changes in irrigation water abstraction generally follow the same direction as changes in irrigated areas, although not proportionally (Figure 4.6). Changes in irrigated areas explain about 20% of changes in irrigation water withdrawals (Annex Figure 4.B.1). In some OECD countries – such as Australia, France, Israel and the United States[3] – use of irrigation water decreased faster than irrigated areas, indicating significant decreases in water application rates (i.e. the national average quantity of irrigation water applied per hectare of agricultural land). In countries with an expanding irrigation sector, such as Mexico and Turkey, use of irrigation water is increasing, although more or less rapidly than changes in irrigated areas.

These contrasting trends of water application rates in OECD countries suggest very different water use efficiency landscapes. Even in countries where irrigation is expanding, it seems that water use efficiency remains relatively stable. However, water data (volumes and surfaces) are subject to considerable fluctuations, particularly when related to weather. In the absence of additional elements, it is not possible to further disentangle the relative role of technical progress (increased application efficiency and improved water productivity) from adaptation strategies, such as changing the crop mix.

Figure 4.5. Irrigation accounts for a large share of agricultural water abstraction in OECD countries

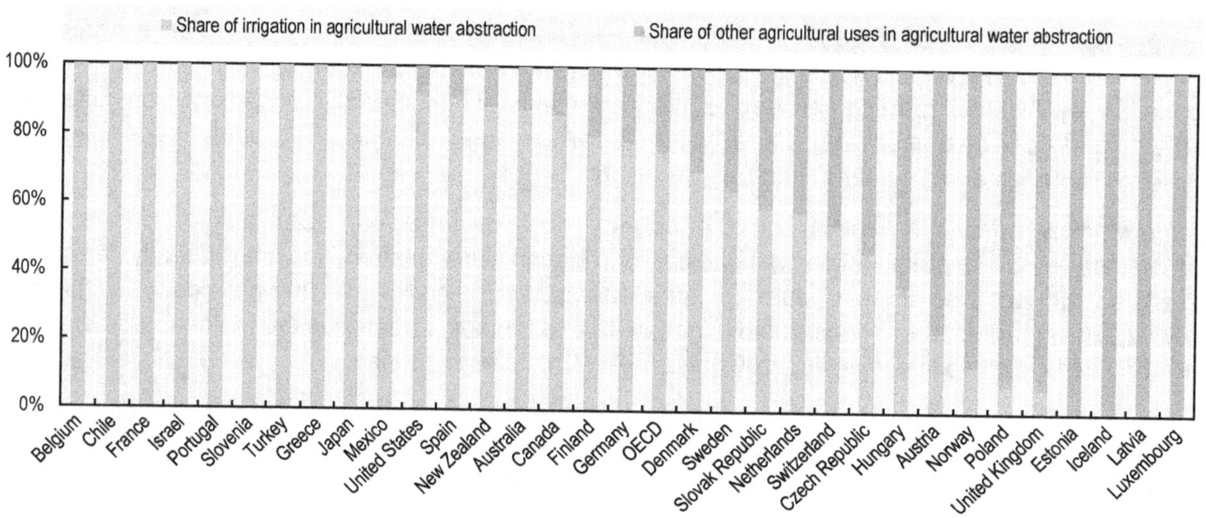

Sources: (OECD, 2016[2]; OECD, 2016[3])

Figure 4.6. Irrigation water abstraction is not just driven by changes in irrigated areas

Average annual percentage change, 2004-06 to 2012-14

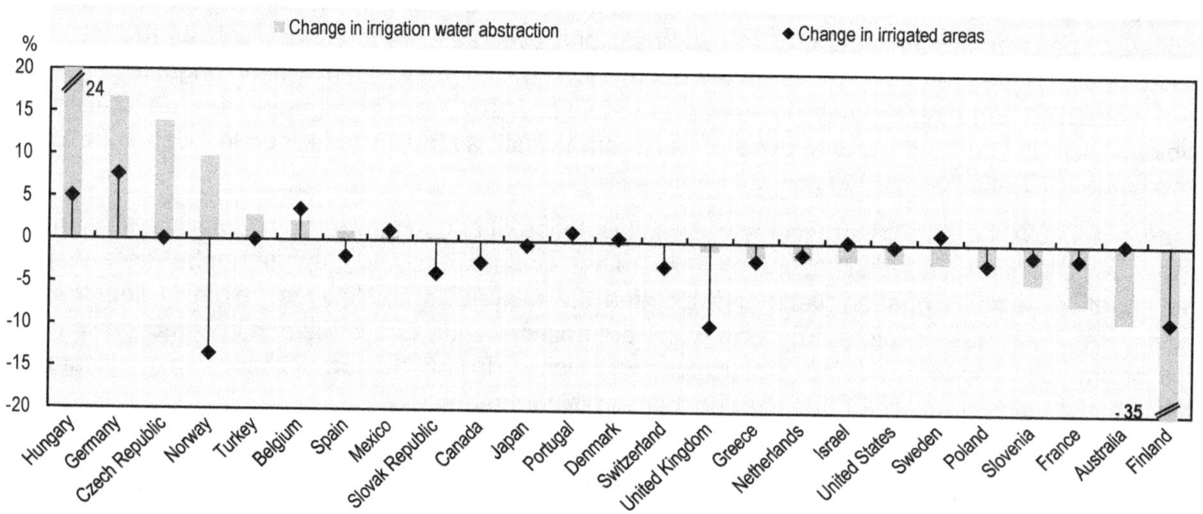

Sources: (OECD, 2016[2]; OECD, 2016[3]).

What drives changes in agricultural water use?

Decoupling agriculture support policies from production decisions and water policy reforms has played an important role, but market drivers are increasing in importance.

Fundamental drivers of changes in agricultural water use include changes in global agricultural markets (e.g. relative prices) and policy drivers (e.g. farm support), but also water regulations including water allocation regimes, water pricing and institutional settings (e.g. governance). Changes in the relative prices of agricultural commodities can lead farmers to change their farming activities (e.g. relative shares of crops and livestock; crop mix). By providing farmers signals of water scarcity, water policies can also motivate them to reconsider their decisions regarding their water use, choice of irrigated areas and freshwater abstraction in the short run, investment decisions in irrigable areas, and equipment modernisation in the long run.

Regarding agricultural policy, the general trend in favour of reduced and decoupled farm support is seen as a positive factor for the proper allocation of resources, including water resources. Prices artificially inflated through government support tend to encourage additional production, and therefore the expansion of irrigation in both area and volume. In several countries, other barriers can limit the influence of decoupling and market prices. Essentially, irrigation requires large-scale investment and specialisation, and can sometimes involve expensive collective hydraulic works that will be recovered only over a long period of time. This may be a source of inertia and limit the extent of agricultural policy reforms.

Several OECD countries have implemented major policy reforms to foster a more efficient and sustainable use of water by agriculture. This is the case of Australia, well known for its water market system. More recently, France has decentralised the management of water rights to local collective management organisms (Unique Organisation of Collective Management), in an effort to improve the efficiency and sharing of water. In Italy, the Italian Association of Local Agencies for the Management of Irrigation Water (ANBI) has developed a web-based irrigation advisory service named "Irriframe" which provides water users with information to improve the efficiency of water use.[4] More generally, over the last ten years the European Union has focused increasingly on the problem of water scarcity, as well as the challenge to integrate water concerns into agricultural policies.

Several challenges remain, however. Agricultural water pricing in the late 2000s remained well below its full cost,[5] and even below operational and maintenance cost recovery in the majority of OECD countries. In some cases, irrigation continues to enjoy substantial public support for, by example, building new hydrological infrastructures. Regulatory approaches are important but not sufficient to provide incentives to use water more efficiently. A growing concern is the lack of efficient groundwater regulations in several OECD countries.

Focus on selected OECD countries

France: Structural changes in the irrigation sector contributed to reducing the use of water in the agricultural sector

France ranks high among OECD countries in terms of reducing irrigation water abstraction over the last decade, with an average annual reduction of about 8%, which was partly due to a decrease in both irrigated areas and water application rates. It is therefore relevant to look at the mechanisms behind these changes.

Weather conditions played a significant role in the decline of irrigation water abstraction. Over the past decade, the national average of rainfall has been relatively higher than usual. Considering that irrigation in France is related to rainfall levels (Commissariat Général au Développement Durable, 2012[6]), higher precipitation may explain in part the decrease in water abstraction. This weather effect may have been more or less pronounced across regions due to different meteorological conditions.

The crop mix in the irrigation sector has evolved significantly. Fifteen years ago, irrigated corn largely dominated other types of irrigated crops, but this area decreased by 17%, from 780 923 ha in 2000 to 645 995 ha in 2010 (Loubier, Campardon and Morardet, 2013[7]). France also witnessed during this period, although to a lesser extent, a reduction in irrigated forages, permanent pastures, potatoes, and protein crops. At the same time, irrigated areas of cereals (wheat, rice, sorghum), notably spring cereals, expanded considerably from 96 351 ha in 2000 to 273 298 ha in 2010 (Loubier, Campardon and Morardet, 2013[7]) (Figure 4.7).

Such important changes in irrigated crop mix have likely contributed to reducing agricultural water abstraction. Indeed, corn typically consumes more water per hectare than other cereals on average, and irrigation of spring cereals comes at a time when rainfall is more abundant and soil moisture is significant. Hence, irrigation essentially complements water needs when net precipitation is not sufficient.

Several drivers simultaneously pushed this change in the irrigated sector in the same direction: reform of the Common Agricultural Policy (CAP), market prices, and environmental regulations. The important switch from corn to spring cereals is probably due to the evolution of the relative prices of corn and other cereals, which have declined for corn since 2005. The CAP reform reduced distortive forms of support that incentivised irrigated maize production. In addition to these market and policy drivers, more frequent water restrictions by water management authorities have probably incited farmers to switch to spring cereals, as these are irrigated during a time period which is less prone to water restrictions imposed by French authorities.

Figure 4.7. Structural change in irrigated crop mix in France, between 2000 and 2010

Share of total irrigated area

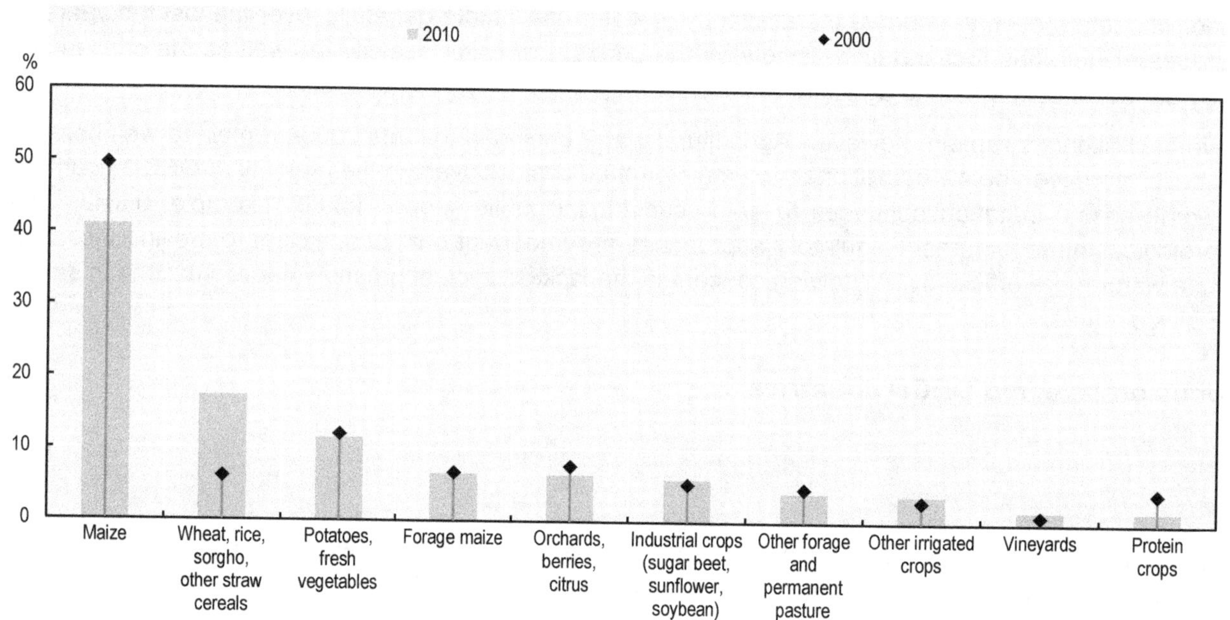

Source: (Loubier, Campardon and Morardet, 2013[7]).

United States: Water use efficiency has improved rapidly, but water scarcity, droughts, groundwater, and competing water use remain significant challenges

In the United States, irrigated farms account for almost 40% of the value of US agricultural production (Schaible and Aillery, 2012[8]). Although irrigation is concentrated in a limited number of states, mainly in the western part of the United States (Nebraska, California, Texas, Idaho, and Colorado), it also plays a large role in several eastern and southern states (Arkansas and Florida). The main irrigated crops include corn (for grain), forage, wheat, rice, and cotton (Schaible and Aillery, 2012[8]). Water rights play a major role in regulating the use of water in the country.

At the national level, water stress has changed little due to the relative stabilisation of total water withdrawals. However, a series of droughts in recent years has highlighted water scarcity issues and the vulnerability of certain agricultural systems to extreme weather events. In California, the reduced availability of groundwater resources during a multiyear drought triggered a major reform (OECD, 2017[9]).

Over the last 20 years, the United States has significantly modernised its irrigation equipment, resulting in increased water use efficiency. Indeed, in the Western United States, the share of irrigated areas using efficient sprinkler and drip or trickle equipment almost doubled between 1994 and 2008, while the area using less efficient irrigation technologies decreased (Figure 4.8).

Figure 4.8. Uptake of efficient irrigation techniques increased substantially in the United States, 1994 – 2008

Share of irrigated area in 17 Western states by irrigation type

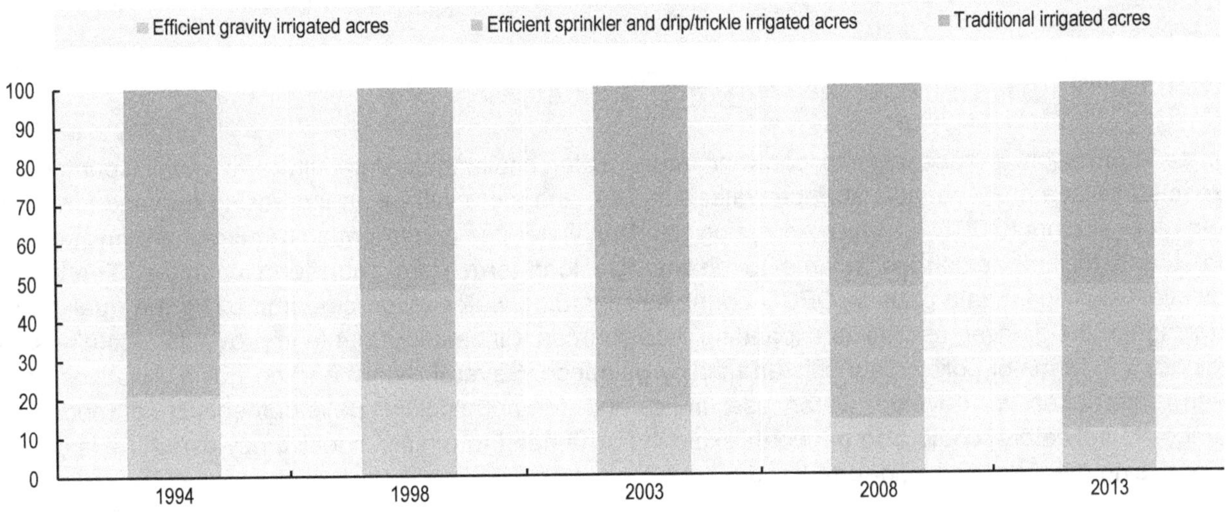

Source: (Schaible and Aillery, 2012[8]).

Investment in irrigation technologies, as well as more frequent extreme weather events such as droughts are the driving forces to greater water use efficiency. Investment in irrigation infrastructure is growing strongly: from USD 2.15 billion in 2008 to USD 2.64 billion in 2013, an increase of 22%. This could also induce additional gains in water use efficiency in the future (Schaible and Aillery, 2012[8]). Several support programmes have played a role in increasing this investment, particularly the Environmental Quality Incentives Program (EQIP). However, although government support can have a leveraging effect, the share of private investment remains dominant (Schaible and Aillery, 2012[8]). Recent droughts may have encouraged farmers to revise their beliefs on the possibility of facing water shortages and prompted tighter legislation on water allocation in some states. These factors could contribute to accelerating the uptake of more efficient irrigation technologies, while avoiding the "rebound effect"[6] that can arise with more efficient water use.

Turkey: Expanding irrigated areas and improving irrigation water use efficiency

Irrigation is an important part of the agricultural sector in Turkey, both historically and economically. Water stress has been increasing (Figure 4.1) due mainly to an increase in water abstraction for agriculture and a proactive policy objective to expand irrigated areas. Climate change is likely to increase further water stress, especially in the southern provinces. Irrigation is at the crossroads of productivity and sustainability issues in Turkey. On the one hand, it is estimated that irrigation could significantly increase yields in areas where it is expanding, but on the other, increased water stress, climate change and increasing competition between industrial and urban uses constitute rising risks for sustainable water allocation (Cakmak, 2010[10]; Özerol and Bressers, 2015[11]; Sen, 2013[12]).

The expansion of irrigated areas is likely to increase pressure on water resources, but there are initiatives to improve and modernise water management. Reforms to decentralise water management from the central administration to local irrigation users have had positive, though limited, impact in improving water management. The uptake of more efficient irrigation techniques has also accelerated over the last decade (OECD, 2015[4]).

However, incentives related to agricultural policies might partly offset these water policy improvements. Turkey uses the most distorting form of support to the agricultural sector. In the period 2013-15, market price support and payments based on outputs and inputs represented 88% of the producer support estimate in the country.[7] The interaction between these various drivers of change will determine the county's path towards sustainable agricultural water management (OECD, 2016[13]).

4.4. Improving water use and irrigation indicators

Better information is necessary to confront future water challenges. Agriculture in many countries is expected to face more variable surface water supplies, and there will be an increasing demand for water from other sectors (OECD, 2017[9]). Analysing trends in water use and irrigation requires harmonised data that are sufficiently extended in time to disentangle long-term from short-term changes. There are, however, significant data gaps in OECD countries regarding water resources. Improving the quality and coverage of the dataset, as well as expanding data sources will be important to improve the usefulness of indicators in terms of policy diagnosis and policy guidance. Several recent and on-going initiatives have been undertaken to develop water use indicators. Methodological developments (e.g. modelling, composite indicators) could also be worth exploring. The need to ensure consistency over time is critical to analysing medium- and long-term trends.

Developing water balances could improve our understanding of water scarcity problems and the tailoring of policy remedies. The water stress indicator has limitations and it would be valuable to improve the measurement of water resource pressures through, for example, a better understanding of the drivers of change in surface and groundwater abstractions and water supply stocks, improving the measurement of water volumes, having basin-scale measurements, and improving consistency across reporting measures by countries. A way to move forward would be to develop water balance accounts, i.e. a comprehensive and consistent account of water stocks and flows in a given water system. The European Commission is attempting to achieve this through its recently released Guidance Document on the application of water balances for supporting the implementation of the Water Framework Directive. Progress in this area could help disentangle policy, market and environmental drivers of change to improve policy guidance for sustainable water management.

Regionalised and geo-localised water data could also be useful for policy makers. Appropriate spatial scale is an important issue for sound analysis of water resources and uses. National averages provide interesting insights about the state and trends of water use in agriculture, but situations vary a great deal across regions and watersheds. Efforts to regionalise water statistics, such as the ones undertaken by Eurostat, could help refine policy analysis and help to better respond to critical water risks (OECD, 2017[9]). For example, the Italian Ministry of Agriculture has a reference WebGIS database for the irrigation sector (National Information System for Water Management in Agriculture – SIGRIAN) that is used to address water management policies.

Big data and satellite images could help to improve water management and monitoring. In recent years there has been an impressive surge in the development and adoption of the last wave of New Technologies of Information and Communication (NTIC) in numerous economic sectors, and agriculture is projected to be an important market in this regard (Kooistra, Van der Wal and Poppe, 2015[14]). The use of big data in agriculture could play an important role in reducing yield gaps (the difference between actual and potential yields), improve environmental performances and the monitoring of water use.

Notes

[1] In the case of France, for example, Amigues et al. (2006[20]) distinguish four irrigation categories: necessary input for production; yield securing in case of drought; yield smoothing over time; and ensuring the quality of crop production.

[2] In several countries, a significant share of agricultural water abstraction is returned to the natural water system (surface and groundwater) as "return flows". This is the case, for example, of the Po Valley in northern Italy.

[3] While the decrease in water application rates observed in the United States is mainly due to improved efficiency and shifts in crop patterns, it should be noted that this trend reflects a shift in regional acreage, with generally less irrigable land in the arid West and acreage expansion in the more humid Eastern states, with lower water application rates.

[4] After four years of activity, Irriframe covers most of the Italian irrigable areas (more than 7 million ha).

[5] The full cost recovery of water includes operating and maintenance and investment costs (capital costs), as well as the cost of water scarcity and externalities (water pollution).

[6] The rebound effect is an economic mechanism initially described by William S. Jevons. It provides that an increase in the efficiency of the use of a resource — through technological progress — could increase the consumption of this resource, rather than decrease it. For example, increasing water use efficiency could increase crop yields, incentivising farmers to use more water by expanding irrigated areas.

[7] Since August 2017, the Turkish government no longer provides market price support to maize in sub-provinces experiencing groundwater deficiency or water scarcity, with the exception of drip irrigated maize. Investment in drip irrigation systems receive support.

References

Amigues, J. et al. (2006), *Sécheresse et agriculture : Réduire la vulnérabilité de l'agriculture à un risque accru de manque d'eau*, Expertise scientifique collective, Rapport, INRA (France), http://inra.dam.front.pad.wedia-group.com/ressources/afile/234277-0c2de-resource-expertise-secheresse-sommaire.html. [20]

BIO Intelligence Service (2012), *Water Saving Potential in Agriculture in Europe: Findings from the Existing Studies and Application to Case Studies*, European Commission DG Env, https://ec.europa.eu/environment/water/quantity/pdf/BIO_Water%20savings%20in%20agicult ure_Final%20report.pdf. [5]

Cakmak, E. (2010), *Agricultural Water Pricing: Turkey*, OECD Publishing, Paris, http://dx.doi.org/10.1787/787034266022. [10]

Commissariat Général au Développement Durable (2012), "Les prélèvements d'eau en France en 2009 et leurs évolutions depuis dix ans", *Observation et statistiques* 290, https://www.eaufrance.fr/sites/default/files/2018-06/prelevements_2009_201202.pdf. [6]

Kenny, J. et al. (2009), "Estimated Use of Water in the United States in 2005", *U.S. Geological Survey Circular*, Vol. 1344, p. 52, https://pubs.usgs.gov/circ/1344/. [16]

Kooistra, L., T. Van der Wal and K. Poppe (2015), "The Role of New Data Sources in Greening Growth: The Case of Drones", *OECD Green Growth and Sustainable Development Forum Session 3*, https://issuu.com/oecd.publishing/docs/ggsd_2015_issuepaper3_final. [14]

Loubier, S., M. Campardon and S. Morardet (2013), "L'irrigation diminue-t-elle en France ? Premiers enseignements du recensement agricole de 2010", *Sciences, Eaux et Territoires*, Vol. 2/11, https://www.cairn.info/revue-sciences-eaux-et-territoires-2013-2-page-12.htm#. [7]

Mekonnen, M. and A. Hoekstra (2016), "Four Billion People Facing Severe Water Scarcity", *Science Advances*, Vol. 2/2, https://advances.sciencemag.org/content/2/2/e1500323. [21]

OECD (2017), *Water Risk Hotspots for Agriculture*, OECD Studies on Water, OECD Publishing, Paris, https://dx.doi.org/10.1787/9789264279551-en. [9]

OECD (2016), "Environment Statistics: Water", *OECD Agriculture Statistics*, https://doi.org/10.1787/agr-data-en. [2]

OECD (2016), "Environmental Performance of Agriculture", *OECD Agriculture Statistics (database)*, http://dx.doi.org/10.1787/data-00660-en. [3]

OECD (2016), *Innovation, Agricultural Productivity and Sustainability in Turkey*, OECD Food and Agricultural Reviews, OECD Publishing, Paris, https://dx.doi.org/10.1787/9789264261198-en. [13]

OECD (2015), *Drying Wells, Rising Stakes: Towards Sustainable Agricultural Groundwater Use*, OECD Studies on Water, OECD Publishing, Paris, https://dx.doi.org/10.1787/9789264238701-en. [4]

OECD (2013), *OECD Compendium of Agri-environmental Indicators*, OECD Publishing, Paris, https://dx.doi.org/10.1787/9789264186217-en. [18]

OECD (2010), *OECD Review of Agricultural Policies: Israel 2010*, OECD Review of Agricultural Policies, OECD Publishing, Paris, https://dx.doi.org/10.1787/9789264079397-en. [19]

OECD (2010), *Sustainable Management of Water Resources in Agriculture*, OECD Studies on Water, OECD Publishing, Paris, https://dx.doi.org/10.1787/9789264083578-en. [1]

OECD (2008), *Environmental Performance of Agriculture in OECD Countries Since 1990*, OECD Publishing, Paris, https://dx.doi.org/10.1787/9789264040854-en. [15]

Özerol, G. and H. Bressers (2015), "Scalar alignment and sustainable water governance: The case of irrigated agriculture in Turkey", *Enviromental Science and Policy*, Vol. 45, pp. 1-10. [11]

Rijsberman, F. (2006), "Water scarcity: Fact or fiction?", *Agricultural Water Management*, Vol. 80/1-3, pp. 5-22, http://dx.doi.org/10.1016/j.agwat.2005.07.001. [17]

Schaible, G. and M. Aillery (2012), "Water Conservation in Irrigated Agriculture: Trends and Challenges in the Face of Emerging Demands", *Economic Information Bulletin*, Vol. No. (EIB-99), p. 67, https://www.ers.usda.gov/publications/pub-details/?pubid=44699. [8]

Sen, Ö. (2013), *A Holistic View of Climate Change and its Impact in Turkey*, Sabanci University, https://ipc.sabanciuniv.edu/wp-content/uploads/2012/11/A-Holistic-View-of-Climate-Change-and-Its-Impacts-in-Turkey.pdf. [12]

Annex 4.A. Description of indicators

The indicators used in this Chapter are the following:

- Irrigation area (hectares)
- Irrigable land area (hectares)
- Agricultural water withdrawals: groundwater, surface water, and total (million m³)
- Irrigation water withdrawals: groundwater, surface water, and total (million m³)
- National water withdrawals (million m³)
- National groundwater withdrawals (million m³)
- National surface water withdrawals (million m³)
- Water stress, defined as the ratio of total freshwater abstractions (all sectors included) to total renewable water resources in the country (%)

The term "agricultural water abstraction" as used here refers to irrigation and other agricultural abstractions (e.g. for livestock) from rivers, lakes, reservoirs and groundwater (shallow wells and deep aquifers), but excludes precipitation directly onto agricultural land. "Water abstraction" is different from "water consumption" in that the latter refers to water depleted and not available for re-use.[1]

For most countries, irrigation freshwater abstraction usually includes water that is applied by an irrigation system to sustain plant growth, including arable, horticultural crops and pasture. Irrigation also includes water that is applied for other beneficial uses — pre-irrigation, frost protection, application of chemicals, weed control, field preparation, crop cooling, harvesting, dust suppression, leaching salts from the root zone — as well as water lost in conveyance (OECD, 2008[15]; Kenny et al., 2009[16]). For some countries, irrigation may cover golf courses, parks, and other non-agricultural uses, and include self-supplied withdrawals and deliveries from private or government companies, districts, and co-operatives.

The indicators related to agriculture water use and irrigation have several limitations which need to be taken into account when examining absolute levels, trends, and comparing countries. The main limitations are: i) cross-country methodological variations in terms of data collection and estimation; ii) cross-country differences in scope (e.g. inclusion of recycled wastewater or not); iii) challenges in monitoring water abstraction, especially for groundwater; and iv) incomplete series of data.

The indicator of water stress is defined as the ratio of total freshwater abstractions (all sectors included) to total renewable water resources in the country. While the indicator is widely used to monitor water resources pressures it has limitations since it does not consider how much water is actually used and not returned to the environment (Rijsberman, 2006[17]). Hence, it may be an imperfect indicator of water scarcity. For this analysis, OECD developed a water stress indicator by combining OECD agri-environmental indicators on water withdrawals by agriculture and estimated renewable freshwater resources from the OECD environmental indicators.

It is important to note that national water indicators may be less meaningful in the case of large countries characterised by a high diversity of climatic zones, hydrologic regimes, and water demands. A country-scale indicator may mask serious water-stress conditions at the basin-level scale.[2]

In this chapter, the trends for the indicators are calculated for the periods 2004-06 to 2012-14. This is to smooth out year-to-year variations. Where needed, other approaches are used to observe the trends in order to ensure a sound interpretation of data. Water withdrawals data vary widely due to meteorological conditions, so trends should be interpreted with caution. When data were not available for 2004-06 or 2012-14, the closest available data were used.

Annex Box 4.A.1. Limitations and challenges of agricultural water use and irrigation indicators

Methods to collect and calculate the data vary across and within countries, and are subject to measurement errors. Sources of data for irrigation include sample surveys of irrigators, and are sometimes estimated using information on irrigated crop acreages along with specific crop water-consumption coefficients or irrigation-system application rates. In other cases, irrigation water withdrawal data may reflect water allocations, which may differ substantially from actual withdrawals depending on annual climatic conditions. These estimates may or may not include adjustments for climatic variables, system efficiencies, conveyance losses, and other irrigation practices such as pre-irrigation (Kenny et al., 2009[16]). The reliability of surveys is also subject to sampling errors, because not all farms are included in the surveys. In many cases, water withdrawals and water used are not closely metered, and farmers may not know themselves precisely how much irrigation water they withdraw.

Data coverage can vary between countries. It is assumed in this chapter that water withdrawals are only from freshwater sources – although recycled wastewater and desalinated water is also used by agriculture in some regions – despite comprising a relatively small proportion of total agriculture withdrawals. For example, saline water use in the United States represented 15% of total water withdrawals in 2005, but nearly all of this was used by the power sector (Kenny et al., 2009[16]). Israel is a notable exception; in 2008, 54% of water resources allocated to agriculture derived from recycled effluent and desalinated water in 2008 (OECD, 2015[4]).

There are practical difficulties in accurately measuring agricultural water withdrawals, especially for groundwater. Groundwater withdrawals on farms, either from shallow wells or deep aquifers, can be difficult to monitor since in most cases groundwater withdrawals are not metered.

Most OECD countries have incomplete series of data for total and agricultural water abstraction and irrigated and irrigable areas (see https://stats.oecd.org/BrandedView.aspx?oecd_bv_id=env-data-en&doi=data-00602-en). In part, this is because these data are usually not calculated annually but obtained from surveys conducted every five or even ten years

Source: (OECD, 2013[18]).

Notes

[1] Water abstraction in Canada provides an illustrative example of the application of these terms, where it is estimated that 70-80% of the water withdrawn is consumed (OECD, 2010[1]).

[2] Having water data and measuring water stress at the basin-level and aggregating at the national level would constitute an improvement. However, this would require common methodologies for the aggregation phase to ensure comparability across countries.

Annex 4.B. Changes in irrigated areas and irrigation water use

Annex Figure 4.B.1. Changes in irrigated area versus changes in irrigation water abstraction

Average annual percentage change, 2005-2014

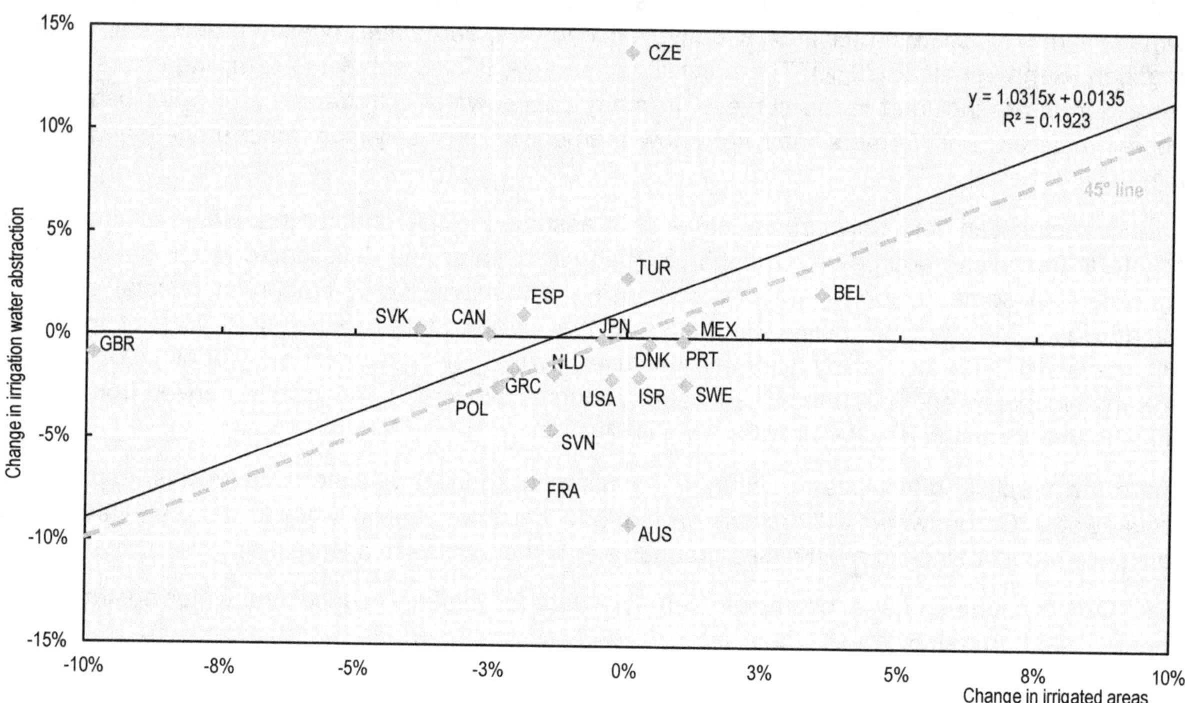

Sources: (OECD, 2016[2]; OECD, 2016[3]).